# Total Quality Management: *A Supervisor's Handbook*

Date Due

Written by Debra L. Morehouse
Edited by National Press Publications

NATIONAL PRESS PUBLICATIONS
A Division of Rockhurst College Continuing Education Center, Inc.
6901 West 63rd Street • P.O. Box 2949 • Shawnee Mission, Kansas 66201-1349
1-800-258-7248 • 1-913-432-7757

National Seminars endorses non-sexist language. However, in an effort to make this handbook clear, consistent and easy to read, we've used the generic "he" when referring to both males and females throughout. The copy is not intended to be sexist.

***Total Quality Management: A Supervisor's Handbook***
© 1992 National Press Publications
A Division of Rockhurst College Continuing Education Center, Inc.

Printed in the United States of America

1   2   3   4   5   6   7   8   9   10

ISBN 1-55852-079-1

# TABLE OF CONTENTS

TQM: OVERVIEW OF MODERN QUALITY
PRINCIPLES AND PRACTICES ................................................ 1

TQM: ORIGIN OF MODERN QUALITY
PRINCIPLES AND PRACTICES ............................................... 13

THE QUALITY GURUS ............................................................ 19

CURRENT STATE OF THE QUALITY MOVEMENT ............ 53

WHAT COMPANIES ARE SAYING ABOUT TQM ................ 79

OPTIONS FOR THE FUTURE .................................................. 89

READINGS .............................................................................. 93

INDEX .................................................................................. 103

# 1

# TQM: OVERVIEW OF MODERN QUALITY PRINCIPLES AND PRACTICES

## WHAT IS TQM?

Total Quality Management (TQM) refers to a management process and a set of disciplines that are coordinated to ensure that the organization consistently meets and exceeds customer requirements. TQM engages all divisions, departments and levels of the organization. Top management makes a commitment to organize all of its strategy and operations around customer needs, and to develop and sustain a culture with high employee participation. TQM companies are focused on the systematic management of data in the elimination of waste and the pursuit of continuous improvement in all processes and practices.

The goal is to deliver the highest value for the customer at the lowest cost, while achieving reasonable profit and economic stability for the company. Top management must commit to a vision and align and train its employees to achieve a common mission.

Cross-functional teams work on improvements responsive to customer requirements. Long-term relationships with customers, suppliers and employees which are focused on quality and not short-term profit are key.

To the question "What is quality?" Zen philosophy responds that there is no answer. It is not definable. Therefore, one is advised to "search for it lovingly."

Robert Pirsig in *Zen and the Art of Motorcycle Maintenance* wondered, perhaps, if it was not "better to travel than to arrive."

As companies embark on a journey in Total Quality Management, these comments may be taken as sage advice. Most likely, a change in the organization's culture will have to occur because TQM will alter the way a company thinks about work and all relationships and interdependencies within the company. TQM will impact every function, system and person connected with the company.

## WHAT DOES TQM MEAN TO YOU?

As managers and supervisors, you are on the front lines of innovation in business and industry today. Both top management and the people you direct look to you for guidance in how to make necessary improvements. Small-business owners are in the same position in directing their employees. The world of work has changed dramatically from an era when all orders came down from the "top" with a due date. Global competition and advances in technology have created market conditions that make all projects and programs seem "past due" before they are even out of the gate.

Your job in working in or creating a TQM environment is to accept the challenge of delivering innovation and improvements in how your company accomplishes its work. How you understand the needs of your customers — both those inside and outside the company — and how you align and develop resources — both human and technical — to meet customer requirements will make all the difference in your company's success.

The results you and your employees deliver will turn company heads faster than any rhetoric about TQM. Learning the principles and practices of Total Quality Management will help you achieve outstanding results and enlist the support of top management in advancing TQM within the organization. From the level of an area manager or supervisor, you can influence "change at the top" and create a work environment that gets the best from its workers.

## SELF-AWARENESS TQM CHECKLIST

TQM has evolved during the past 50 years and combines management approaches from organizational, technical and humanistic frameworks. Probably some of what you and your company already do reflects TQM principles and practices. Use the TQM checklist to rate your company and yourself on TQM applications on a scale from 1 - 5 based on the following criteria. Each item is worth five points, with five representing the greatest TQM strength in a given area. The highest possible score you can achieve is 50 in rating TQM readiness, 25 points each for both the company and its managers and supervisors.

## RATING SCALE

### 1. No Awareness/No Application
No awareness of TQM principles and no applications

### 2. Minimal Awareness/Minimal Application
Some awareness, but little application or follow-through in an area or department

### 3. Evolving Awareness/Some Application
Evolving awareness, and some application and follow-through in an area or department

**4. Established Awareness/Some Integration**
Established awareness, some application and follow-through, but limited integration and use within the company

**5. Comprehensive Awareness/Full Integration**
Comprehensive awareness and integration of TQM principles and practices throughout the company

## SELF-AWARENESS TQM CHECKLIST

1. No Awareness/No Application
2. Minimal Awareness/Minimal Application
3. Evolving Awareness/Some Application
4. Established Awareness/Some Integration
5. Comprehensive Awareness/Full Integration

## YOUR COMPANY

1. The mission and goals of the company are clear.  _____

2. Top management communicates in a timely and purposeful way with employees about the "big picture" — new products, growth, market share, achievements and problems.  _____

3. The company is driven by quality.  _____

4. The company is focused on customer needs.  _____

5. The company provides clear incentives for employees to seek improvements and innovations.  _____

### TOTAL COMPANY SCORE
(Highest Possible Score = 25)  _____

## SELF-AWARENESS TQM CHECKLIST

1. No Awareness/No Application
2. Minimal Awareness/Minimal Application
3. Evolving Awareness/Some Application
4. Established Awareness/Some Integration
5. Comprehensive Awareness/Full Integration

## MANAGERS/SUPERVISORS IN YOUR COMPANY

1. There are active and effective cross-functional teams working on process improvements.     _____

2. Communication is open, people are respected and trust is the norm.     _____

3. Managers and supervisors regularly initiate new ideas and practices and serve as a positive link between top management and employees.     _____

4. Managers and supervisors are committed to developing both themselves and their people.     _____

5. Managers and supervisors, together with their employees, create regular avenues for customer interaction and input.

    _____

**TOTAL MANAGERS/SUPERVISORS SCORE**
(Highest Possible Score = 25)     _____

## INTERPRETING THE RESULTS

Now that you have rated the TQM readiness of your company and its managers and supervisors, you have a better idea of how well-focused you are on meeting the needs of your customers. You probably have a better idea of how well-integrated your company is with communication, existing operations and systems, and the level of commitment management has to innovation and improvements.

You may be asking, "What can I do as a manager or supervisor to increase TQM awareness and activity in my immediate work environment?" Everyone needs to start somewhere. Frequently, changes to "how the job gets done" come from that part of an organization which has the greatest autonomy. That gives managers and supervisors a great deal of room to influence attitudes, values and behaviors.

Today, creative managers and supervisors in American industry are taking on leadership responsibility to introduce TQM principles and practices up and down the production chain. Continuous and incremental improvements are happening through an ongoing series of small steps. These managers and supervisors are energizers in bringing the right issues to their bosses and peers. They are focused on adding value for customers and saving money for their companies.

The material in this handbook will help you become a champion in your role as a TQM manager or supervisor. Review the TQM Checklist again to get a solid picture of how TQM principles are applied in practice. You will also find several sections very helpful in describing "what companies look like" that practice TQM. Refer especially to sections on:

- "How TQM Practices and Principles Can Improve My Performance"
- "TQM Companies vs. Traditional Companies"
- "How TQM Companies Work"
- "TQM Readiness Quiz"
- "Culture Change and Shifting Paradigms"

## YOUR FIRST RESPONSIBILITY — DEVELOPING PEOPLE

The most influential factors for job satisfaction are positive work relationships and mastery of the knowledge and skills essential for doing the job. The single most significant relationship in determining "success on the job" is an employee's relationship to his boss. As a manager or supervisor, your critical role as "boss" is to develop people to contribute their best.

As a small-business owner, manager or supervisor, your first responsibility is to guide people in producing the best results possible for the company. You need to train and coach people to master the knowledge and skills required to excel in their jobs, and to master your own style of interpersonal communication with people.

First, you need to understand the vision and mission of your organization. Second, you need to develop a working style and incentives that produce "action steps" among your employees, co-workers and even your boss. Together these create customer-driven, high-quality operations and processes. To do this, you must learn about the unique talents and concerns of the people with whom you work — particularly your subordinates. Learn what motivates them, how each seeks his own performance improvement and how you can help.

## "MANAGING UP" — GETTING "BUY IN" FROM YOUR BOSS

Frequently, managers and supervisors complain that their bosses do not understand what it takes for them to achieve success. Sometimes bosses themselves are lacking in their own abilities to lead, manage and communicate effectively. However, the fact remains that real work must be accomplished with greater and greater precision and quality. TQM environments require that managers and supervisors learn how to communicate in all directions within their organizations, directing and influencing the work of those around them — superiors, subordinates and peers.

Granted, this commitment to "get smart" about managing your boss is a tall order. It is aimed at agreement on a scope of responsibilities and "what success looks like." However, neglecting communication around such vital concerns keeps you operating in a vacuum. Early agreement or "buy in" from your boss will make later negotiations for such items as process improvements and requests for additional resources more obtainable.

Bosses do not necessarily take the lead in communication, yet the need exists to build alliances. Therefore, front-line managers and supervisors must be willing to develop skills to address this challenge. It is an essential first step in strengthening their own position and authority in developing a TQM culture of high employee participation among their subordinates and co-workers.

## HOW TQM PRACTICES AND PRINCIPLES CAN IMPROVE YOUR PERFORMANCE

Review the following list to see how your performance as a small-business owner, manager or supervisor will improve by putting the principles of TQM to work with your company's employees. Place one of the following numbers in front of each item to demonstrate your strength in your current TQM practices.

1. Aware but not active
2. Aware but lacking in "know-how"
3. Active with some applications
4. Leading in my department but not linking with peers or boss
5. Leading in my department and linking with peers and boss

Your goal is to progress from 1 to 5 in each area. This list will help you identify barriers to achieving this progression and help you tackle the key issues that prevent your full success as a TQM manager or supervisor.

## VISION, MISSION, GOALS

_____Align your understanding with that of your boss and your subordinates.

____Keep employees informed about the company's achievements — market share, growth, new product development, competitor position.

____Help employees link their daily efforts with the company's goals.

## CUSTOMER SATISFACTION (INTERNAL AND EXTERNAL)

____Survey and capture customer feedback to current products and services delivered by your people.

____Communicate with customers to discover improvements and upgrades to products, services and processes.

____Provide analysis of customer feedback and seek adjustments in current systems and service.

## EMPLOYEE PARTICIPATION/TRAINING

____Learn about each employee's strengths and weaknesses and what expectations each has for his own performance.

____Set company-related individual goals and objectives with each employee to maximize performance and set standards for excellence.

____Empower employees to seek improvements to processes and systems around them.

____Provide training in communications, team problem-solving and TQM principles and tools.

## TEAM SYNERGY/PROCESS IMPROVEMENTS

____Establish a baseline of current productivity, set goals for improvements in systems and performance, and create measurement systems which employees can use to track progress.

_____Create cross-functional teams to "troubleshoot" improvements in work-process flows, operational systems and measurement, with the goals of adding value for the customer and eliminating waste.

_____Establish rewards and incentives that recognize both individual contributions and the impact of team effort.

## TQM COMPANIES VS. TRADITIONAL COMPANIES

### QUALITY AND VALUE ARE WHAT THE CUSTOMER PERCEIVES THEM TO BE

Companies that subscribe to TQM focus their strategy, their operations and their employees on "listening to the customer." Understanding who makes up the customer base and the various market segments within that base provides companies with the best clues of how to maintain and expand market share and to delegate resources for growth in areas where true market needs exist. The following characteristics contrast TQM companies with those whose practices hasten their obsolescence.

- Customer-Driven vs. Company-Driven

- Total Customer Service vs. Customer Satisfaction at Less Than 100%

- Long-Term Commitment vs. Short-Term Profitability

- Continuous Improvement vs. Completion on Time at Any Cost

- Elimination of Waste vs. High Cost

- High Quality and Low Cost vs. Low Quality and High Cost

- Quality at the Source vs. Inspection After the Fact

- Leading People and Measuring Things vs. Measuring Performance

- Cross-Functional Teams vs. Highly-structured Departments

- High Employee Participation vs. Top-Down Hierarchy

- Multilevel Communication vs. Formal Channels of Top-Down Communication

## HOW TQM COMPANIES WORK

Companies that utilize a TQM philosophy share the following traits:

- Common vision and shared values communicated throughout the organization, focusing employees and customers on the company's mission

- Trust and open communication nurtured and rewarded

- Top-level commitment for TQM throughout the organization

  - Effective internal leadership at contractor and principal subcontractor levels

  - Continuous improvement of all processes; quality first before schedule and profit; development of a common language for continuous-improvement philosophy and strategies

  - Integrated hardware and software systems and services to support the stream from customer requirements, to conformance, to continuous improvement, to total customer satisfaction

- Cultural and individual support to achieve cultural change so all employees seek new learning and continuous improvement

- Benchmarking: "best practices" that top companies used to improve capacity and productivity

- Training in TQM principles and tools; total customer satisfaction; creative and strategic thinking and planning; problem-solving; resolving conflict; working in teams and participative management; and ongoing training to develop optimum TQM culture

- Broad expectations established by management; creativity and innovation stimulated and rewarded

- Flexible, adaptable work teams and processes that adjust to new product/service requirements and that respond to customer needs and achieve maximum employee participation

- Continuous-improvement methods that are related to specific functions within the organization being worked on by many teams

- Process management, process improvement and process measurement that are fundamental and appropriate for all managers

- Supplier-customer partnerships working on improvements; TQM as a key consideration in source selection; sole-sourcing, having only one vendor per product, offers a competitive strategy to serve the end-customer

- Commitment to research & development

# 2

# TQM: ORIGIN OF MODERN QUALITY PRINCIPLES AND PRACTICES

## TQM AND THE ECONOMIC RECOVERY OF POST-WAR JAPAN

During post-war assessment of Japanese manufacturing, Americans concluded that Japanese engineering wasn't so bad, but Japanese management needed an overhaul. Karou Ishikawa (one of the quality leaders discussed in the "Quality Gurus" section of this handbook) and other Japanese working with him thought the statistical methods and procedures the Americans brought had value. But they determined they would have to adapt American management theories to reflect Japanese norms and culture.

The Japanese have contributed much from their culture to the gifts of statistical methods brought to them by W. Edwards Deming and the strategy of managing for quality brought to them by Joseph Juran. William Ouchi's *Theory Z* (1981) details how the Japanese infused their own roots in developing their own management systems. Many of the most fundamental principles of TQM come from Japanese culture. Trust, long-term commitment, collaboration, emulation, reciprocity, subtlety, and the discipline of incremental and continuous improvement are but a few of TQM's foundation blocks that mirror Japanese culture.

Western management theories, such as Douglas McGregor's "Theory Y," recognize the creativity and ingenuity of workers and encourage the development of work environments that stimulate and reward such individual contributions. It was the Japanese, however, who first understood contributions had to come from all workers at all levels, and the rewards had to be shared among all the contributors in the organization. For example, bonuses paid annually are proportionate to an employee's rate of compensation.

On a following page, refer to the chart "Quality — The Key to Japan's Economic Recovery," which depicts the thinking that has guided top management in Japan since 1950. The Japanese strategy, developed with Deming and Juran, was to deliver better quality at a lower price. Deming predicted Japan's success in the following quote:

> "The year 1950 was the beginning of a new Japan in quality. I predicted in 1950 that Japanese products would within five years invade the markets of the world, and that the standard of living in Japan would in time rise to equality with the world's most prosperous countries.

> "The basis for my confidence in this prediction was:

> (1) observations on the Japanese workforce;
> (2) knowledge and devotion to their jobs of Japanese management;
> (3) faith that Japanese management would accept and carry out their responsibilities;

(4) expansion of education by the Japanese Union of
   Scientists & Engineers (JUSE)."

Dr. Edwards Deming
***Out of the Crisis***
MIT, Second Edition, 1986

**Total Quality Management: An Overview**
**Quality — The Key to Japan's Economic Recovery**

"The following chain reaction was on the blackboard of every top-management meeting in Japan from early 1950 onward."
                                                    — Dr. Deming

| Improve Quality | Costs Decrease | Productivity Improves | Capture the Market | Stay in Business | Provide Jobs and More Jobs |
|---|---|---|---|---|---|

- Less
  rework
- Fewer
  mistakes
- Fewer
  delays
- Better use
  of machine-
  time and
  materials

- Better
  quality
- Lower
  prices

## POST-WAR AMERICAN DOMINANCE AND JAPAN'S EMERGENCE AS AN ECONOMIC SUPERPOWER

During World War II, American companies focused on exactly what they were asked to do by the government — mass production. Never before had any nation in the history of the world called its production forces into such incessant and dedicated production. Quantity and quality were synonymous for "getting the job done right the first time and on schedule."

U.S. military operations required "fail-safe" technology for all strategic vessels and weaponry, as well as highly-sophisticated navigation and communications equipment. The development and application of the most advanced technology the world had ever seen was placed under the most stringent quality research and production standards. Coupled with the demand for continuous production, the military's need for guaranteed precision and accuracy created the backdrop around which the quality movement began.

At the end of World War II, the U.S. controlled a third of the world economy and made half the manufactured goods sold in the world. American industry fueled a peacetime economy through mass production. Quantity was the goal — not specialty markets requiring distinct manufacturing processes. Industry believed it could not slow down to accommodate the few when there were so many others ready to buy the standard. The world was on a consumer binge, and America just kept turning out product.

Top-level corporate executives saw no advantage in pursuing quality over quantity. American management viewed Quality Control as part of engineering for which manufacturing was responsible. The concept of Acceptable Quality Levels (AQL) became the standard for American manufacturing. (AQL calculations were expressed in defects per hundred.) For U.S. firms, quality was an inspection issue. Higher quality standards would mean more inspection, resulting in higher costs. Management thus concluded — incorrectly, as the Japanese have proven — that higher quality would always mean higher costs.

In contrast, the Japanese trained everyone to analyze his job and to seek opportunities to improve how work was done. The Japanese did not lock in their procedures, but took pride in the challenge of perfecting a process by incremental improvements. They began to define quality as a "constant reduction in variability." The Japanese raised their goals steadily and continued to apply the formula they had been displaying since 1950.

The Japanese ability to produce high quality, low cost goods became stronger and stronger. Deming's statistical methods to trim variations to a hairline and Juran's management concepts combined with Ishikawa's "Quality Circles" and Taguchi's "Loss Control Function" to bridle deviance where it begins provided Japanese manufacturers with powerful and competitive tools.

Because the Japanese had been analyzing various U.S. industries since the war, they were eager to compete directly with U.S. companies. They went after American manufacturers, offering superior reliability and lower cost. These were attributes few found easy to refuse in the early 1970s and in the early 1980s.

Japan's strategy was to attack at the low end of the market and build credibility from there. By entering markets at the low end, many Japanese companies generated the volume needed to go after the high-priced market later. When the Japanese went after the higher end of a market, they did so with the same strategy, by offering superior-quality products at lower cost than their U.S. competitors.

There is a long list of U.S. industries that have fallen prey to this strategy: machine tools, automobiles, cameras, diesel engines, steel, VCRs, electronics and advanced computer technology. Japan has been reclaiming its position in the world through a relentless commitment to quality and by chipping away at American market dominance.

The advent of Japanese economic muscle worldwide may have been avoided if the U.S. had chosen the same commitment to higher quality, reduced cost and TQM work environments as Japan did after World War II. U.S. manufacturers were caught asleep at the switch, and as a result, Japan has achieved its current world-class status.

# 3

## THE QUALITY GURUS

### W. EDWARDS DEMING

W. Edwards Deming (1900 -    ), who resides in Washington,
D.C., ranks with General Douglas MacArthur as one of the most
famous Americans in Japan. His contribution to post-war Japan has
been cited as a pivotal factor in the rebuilding of its economy.
Deming provided both a philosophy and a system for applying
statistical methods to achieve higher quality and productivity in
manufacturing and management.

Deming promised the Japanese in the 1950s that the methods
he taught would not only help them rebuild their industries at home
after the war, but would enable them to compete in world markets
in the future. He said Japan would compete through continuous
improvement and the elimination of waste. Higher-quality products
would be produced at lower cost.

Japan had just been devastated by the war and was occupied by the Allied forces. With few natural resources, the Japanese wisely calculated the need to develop their technological intelligence. Deming offered the Japanese hope for their stake in the future. He believed their commitment to quality would help them advance, and so did they.

Research done by Walter Shewhart and his colleagues at Bell Laboratories in the 1930s was the foundation for the development of Statistical Process Control (SPC). Shewhart is credited with combining the principles of quality control with statistics and probabilities to develop Statistical Quality Control.

Shewhart referred Deming to Homer Sarasohn, a Bell Labs colleague, who taught statistical methods in Japan. Sarasohn and Deming were given the task of training the Japanese to produce communications equipment that would allow the occupation forces to inform and educate the nation of its progress during rebuilding. Further, Sarasohn and Deming were given the opportunity to use the communications industry as an example of how the Japanese economy could be revived.

Deming was tenacious about his assignment, and so were the Japanese. Years later, Deming recalled his first class in Japan: "I've never had better students. I'd describe them as the top five percent of all classes I've ever taught."

It was Shewhart's Cycle — Plan, Do, Check and Act (PDCA) — which became the Deming Cycle — Plan, Do, Study and Act (PDSA) — in Japan and provided the logic behind SPC methods. Joseph Juran, also with Bell Labs, was invited by Shewhart to Japan in 1954 after the publication of his book, *Quality Control Handbook* (1951). (Refer to the section "The Shewhart/Deming Cycle" as well as notes on Juran.)

Clearly, other quality experts have provided strong direction and a straightforward style in telling companies what to do. Deming comes more from the camp of teaching people how to fish rather than feeding them. Deming is recognized for pushing organizations the hardest.

Companies that have worked with him explain Deming will probe all the difficult issues in the organization. He is an holistic thinker and doer and will challenge others to work in that framework. Deming understands that in order to change behavior — "We've always done it this way" — an organization will have to rethink its attitudes, beliefs and values.

Today, Japan's most coveted prize recognizing industrial quality is the Deming Award. (Only one American company has won this award — Florida Power and Light in 1989.) Deming also received The Second Order Medal of the Sacred Treasurer in 1960, the highest award Japan can bestow on a foreigner. Today Deming still lectures and teaches his four-day seminar in quality.

## DEMING'S CHALLENGE FOR MANAGEMENT

Deming believes quality is 85 percent the responsibility of management and 15 percent the responsibility of employees. Quality circles, developed in Japan in the late 1950s and early 1960s (based on Western management theories such as Douglas McGregor's "Theory Y"), addressed only the 15 percent that belonged to the employees. Deming developed his Fourteen Points as a "Charter for Management" in order to seek management's commitment and stewardship of quality.

The three key ingredients of Deming's Fourteen Points are:

- Constancy of purpose
- Continual improvement
- Profound knowledge

The Fourteen Points are described in detail in this handbook, where Deming's thoughts on constancy of purpose and continual improvement are represented. While profound knowledge is not one of the Fourteen Points, it is an orientation management needs to embrace when leading a total-quality process.

Deming's concept of profound knowledge sets him apart from the other quality gurus. Profound knowledge exemplifies Deming as philosopher. It demonstrates the underlying core beliefs and values about learning which have guided Japan's economic recovery and rise to world-power status. Deming's philosophy and methods are only now beginning to gain widespread recognition for their impact on quality and productivity in U.S. companies.

Profound knowledge, according to Deming, comprises broad categories:

- appreciation for a system
- theory of variation
- theory of knowledge
- psychology

Deming teaches that these components of knowledge are inseparable. To learn anything, one must commit to the whole.

Appreciation for the system is a starting point. Deming explains that when every part of a system is working in support of another part, "optimization" occurs. To achieve optimization, Deming says all internal competition must be eliminated. Numerical ratings and rankings need to be eliminated in assessing and conveying feedback to an individual about his performance.

Deming makes two points about variation. First, mistakes, defects and variation will always occur. And when something goes wrong, people believe it was caused by random variation or by something specific. Then they often apply the wrong "corrective" action.

Many dollars are wasted as organizations try to understand what has caused a problem. Deming recommends applying the Shewhart/Deming Cycle to analyze a problem and using Shewhart's Control Chart to track activity. The visual representation of behavior will demonstrate if random variation occurs. (As an event occurs, it is plotted at the given juncture on the X and Y axes, each representing a variable such as time and date.)

> (Note: Phil Crosby, on the other hand, disagrees with Deming and believes in Zero Defects. Crosby rejects statistically-based quality methods that accept as inevitable that some things will go wrong at some time. All the rest of the quality experts simply think Crosby is wrong about his concept.)

Deming views knowledge as a prediction that "comes true." He believes that knowledge comes from theory, and without theory there is no learning. Without a theory of knowledge that underlines experience, Deming states an organization cannot learn from its own experience or that of another company. So, one organization cannot simply "copy" another's success in total quality improvement. This also explains why a company cannot formulate a "Total Quality Plan." It is a process, so each company must develop its own.

Psychology, according to Deming, is the most powerful component of the four elements of profound knowledge. He believes people are born with a natural inclination to learn and be innovative. Management unintentionally and frequently works against developing the capacity of its employees. Measurement by rating and ranking people robs them of their intrinsic motivation.

Train the people to measure "things," says Deming, and they will keep pushing their own standards higher to "beat" themselves. Organizations need to recognize that people learn at different rates and in different ways. Training methods and approaches need to increase learning for individuals and for the organization itself.

Deming is both a philosopher and a pragmatist in his approach to quality. He has provided both inspiration and discipline for the human spirit. His life has been dedicated to enhancing productivity and the quality of work life for organizations and individuals. The application of profound knowledge in the practice of TQM has placed customers and suppliers front-and-center to the goals of business.

Like Pirsig in *Zen and the Art of Motorcycle Maintenance* (1976), Deming believes quality is not definable. One knows quality when one experiences it, and one can measure its improvement.

According to Deming, quality is a moving target, and as such is continuously improving because of our changing needs and expectations. Deming seeks "transformational" experiences in the workplace and in individual lives by using discipline and discovery over time.

Deming believes the inherent value of quality is in its pursuit. How managers and supervisors align and motivate their people to contribute their collective efforts to achieve a common goal is quality's real challenge.

## THE SHEWHART/DEMING CYCLE
## PDSA (PDCA) CYCLE
## PLAN, DO, STUDY AND ACT

Total quality and its commitment to continuous improvement requires that work and processes be thought of in a circular system — not as a linear path of beginning, middle and end.

An entire process is analyzed and an aspect of the total process is isolated for improvement. Then, a plan is developed to achieve an improvement. Once the plan is clear, it is enacted. The results of enacting the plan are recorded, studied and assessed. Then, action is taken either to incorporate the improvement into the process because it achieves the desired impact, to rework the change until it meets the mark, or abort the idea and come up with a new one.

In total quality, consensus must be reached and a change must be made in the process. This means all constituents currently are satisfied with the outcome, and the improvement is recognized as a reduction in cost, cycle time and tightened variance of the unexpected. In total quality, the next step is to attack some other aspect in the process and repeat the cycle.

It is important to understand that Plan, Do, Study and Act (PDSA) is a process cycle. Because frequently many people from various departments are involved and they may experience a "breakthrough," a cycle can be thought of as a project. However, it is significant to maintain the perspective of the experience as a cycle, not as a one-time-only "project." Projects can be completed; however, a process can always be improved.

Walter Shewhart conceived this thought pattern in a cycle of Plan, Do, Check and Act (PDCA). Deming modified it to Plan, Do, Study, and Act (PDSA) in 1990. This is called the Deming Cycle in Japan, and either the Shewhart or Deming Cycle in the U.S.

# THE SHEWHART/DEMING CYCLE
# PDSA (PDCA) CYCLE
# PLAN, DO, STUDY AND ACT

**PLAN**    Process improvements can be achieved at any level of organization within a company. Focusing on customer requirements and including input from upstream and downstream suppliers, internal customers and distributors will deliver the best results. Managers and supervisors need to involve employees in troubleshooting the system and planning improvements.

In Japan, the majority of time on a project is spent in planning. In the U.S., the reverse is typically true. The pressure on managers in American companies is to move quickly through planning, then spend excessive time and money in rework. The intent here is if there are 20 days for the entire cycle, 10 should be spent in planning.

**DO**    Once there is an initiative for improvement, it is acted out in a small-scale test. The Deming Cycle is a statistical device and allows employees to record variation and focus on incremental improvements. A manageable scope is identified and, as part of the test, observations are recorded. Tools used to record observations are: flowcharts, cause and effect diagram (Ishikawa Fishbone Diagram), Pareto chart, trend chart, histogram, scatter diagram, and control chart. (See the Seven Basic Tools and the charts.)

**STUDY**    All results from the test are examined and discussed. The impact of elements of the test are thought of in terms of their relationship to all other aspects of the whole. Thorough analysis requires a clear understanding of these interrelationships.

**ACT**    Based on the aims of the test, which were determined during planning, some decision is made to either adopt, adjust or abandon the plan. At this point, employees are back at the top of the cycle and can again follow along the path of continuous improvement.

## The Shewhart Cycle

## DEMING'S 14 POINTS: GUIDING PRINCIPLES OF TOTAL QUALITY

1. **Create constancy of purpose for improvement of product and service.** Deming suggests companies commit to constant improvement, customer satisfaction, research and development, and the development of employees aligned around the company's goals. They should stop focusing on "quick fixes" for short-term profits. Determine what business the company is in and adapt to changing customer needs. Have a purpose beyond making money. Make it your mission.

2. **Adopt the new philosophy.** Americans have tolerated inferior quality in products and services for a long time. Increased global competition is demanding a shift. Deming

challenges companies to approach quality with a new tenacity which insists on error-free work, as well as a management and worker commitment to continually improving products and services.

3. **Cease dependence on mass inspection.** Deming staunchly advocates the education of workers at every step in the development, delivery and evaluation of the work to "troubleshoot" the process. American industry has wasted billions making inferior products and in delivering services that have lost customers and then spent billions more trying to correct the errors and winning customers back.

Typically, inspection has had negative overtones and occurs in isolation after the work has been done. Deming recommends eliminating inspectors and rewarding people for finding errors, stopping the process and improving both the process and quality as work is performed.

4. **End the practice of awarding business on price tag alone.** Deming recommends new thinking in vendor relationships. Instead of awarding work on the lowest bid, which often means the lowest quality, companies need to develop long-term relationships with suppliers, especially sole-source suppliers for any one item. Expect vendors to demonstrate their own TQM. View vendors as business partners and develop mutual respect, trust, responsibility and rewards.

Time spent up-front identifying the goal, planning and selecting a strategy to serve all the customers and clarifying roles and responsibilities will reduce cycle times and errors. Building strategic, quid-pro-quo alliances with suppliers who deliver results over time is a key competitive advantage.

5. **Improve constantly and forever the system of production and service.** Quality requires ongoing commitment to continuous improvement, elimination of waste and reductions in cycle times. Management achieves this by rewarding the creativity and initiative of its employees who try new things and accomplish benefits for customers and gains for the company.

6. **Institute training.** Deming insists many performance problems can be traced to the lack of orientation and training programs. Management needs to set expectations for employees and demonstrate how workers can be successful in their jobs. People want to do a good job; give them the tools.

7. **Institute leadership.** Managers need to lead people and manage things. Managers need to support workers to their fullest potential and adopt the roles of coach, mentor and cheerleader. The organization is in the business it's in, but managers are in the organization business — and that means developing people. A manager's final product is creating an environment in which people can make their best contributions, which result in the organization being productive and successful.

8. **Drive out fear.** These are three small words, but they are perhaps the most potent challenge for management to achieve. Deming correctly states that companies who make it "unsafe" for employees to ask questions and learn to do things right are facing tremendous economic losses on the way to their own obsolescence. Employees who are afraid are not free to create.

9. **Break down barriers between staff areas.** Deming points out the integrity and good sense of why divisions, departments and units need to communicate and work closely with one another. Concurrent design, a standard in

Japan that expects departments to work together from the onset, is increasing in recognition in the U.S. due to its essential contribution to quality, customer satisfaction and profit.

In the service industries, this concept can be applied by integrating planners, systems designers, marketers, financial analysts and customers when services are being developed and process flows are being detailed. Weigh out value price — what the customer perceives as having value and what he is willing to pay for — and value cost — what it costs the company to produce the service. Employees will love collecting this data and making recommendations.

10. **Eliminate slogans, exhortations and targets for the workforce.** Deming rejects hype and superimposed targets, claiming they have no meaning unless they evolve from the workforce. Deming is opposed to competition within, between and among units of the same organization, believing that kind of competition works against the goal of removing internal barriers.

Frequently, hype is employed to foster competition within the company to produce higher productivity and profit. Deming says organizations need to redirect the competitive spirit to their real competitors in the outside business world.

11. **Eliminate numerical quotas.** This is a difficult concept to grasp. Everyone knows that business runs on numbers! Translated to a functional definition, this means that achieving the numbers alone does not mean achieving quality, or maintaining or expanding market share, or providing for innovation in new products and services. Workers who are held to meeting quotas are held to yesterday's standards; they are not moving the company into the future. Worse, quotas merely guarantee workers will do whatever it takes to make the mark. This thinking is

probably directly responsible for the past high defect rate in the U.S. due to the country's commitment to mass production.

12. **Remove barriers to pride of workmanship.** It is management's responsibility to listen to workers to determine what barriers exist to achieving consistently good performance. Deming places a great amount of emphasis on management's role to provide an environment where employees can excel.

    Essential elements include training for managers and for all employees throughout the organization, providing technology and materials which support the accomplishment of strong results, and instituting employee practices and procedures which support worker dedication and achievement.

13. **Institute a vigorous program of training and retraining.** Deming is clear to say adopting a quality program or process will not be easy or quick. The ideal is for the entire organization to be educated in the new methods, including teamwork and statistical techniques.

    Communicating, planning in a group context, negotiating and problem-solving are areas where training occurs early. Deming advises that training occur first top-down for all levels of management to assure that managers and supervisors are aligned behind the same concepts and that they share a common language. Next, those in work groups or project teams on the pilot quality effort are trained in the new methods, teamwork and statistical techniques.

    As many departments and project teams commit to these same principles and create an internal impact for their own areas, they attract the attention of co-workers because of their successes. Change occurs at every juncture and begins to have an impact when there is a critical mass of awareness and practice. Management will notice improvements, especially ones that deliver the results it wants.

Because a commitment to quality is a commitment to improvement, the baseline becomes obvious. Companies rethink who they are and how they want to do business. Typically for most organizations, this is a painful process. It requires insight about one's role in current practices and relationships. New learning and continuous training accompany the route toward continuous improvement.

14. **Take action to accomplish the transformation.** Deming is clear that a special top-management team must develop a plan of action to carry out its quality mission. Total quality is a process that recognizes the total organization as a system, including all internal and external constituents — customers, suppliers and competitors. Once the critical mass of people who comprise the core of the company and its partners understand the Fourteen Points and the Seven Deadly Diseases, they will become aligned and committed to quality.

## DEMING'S SEVEN DEADLY DISEASES

1. **Lack of constancy of purpose.** When a company has no constancy of purpose, no long-range plans exist and management and employees both are insecure. Everyone wonders what they are supposed to do. What is the plan for staying in business? For what purpose is the business organized? This information is significant throughout all departments and in every work group of a company. Managers and supervisors provide a key interface between the company and its workers.

2. **Emphasis on short-term profits.** U.S. business is focused on quarterly reports of profitability that undermine quality and productivity. This obsession has created the misplaced preoccupation with making companies appear to be profitable on paper, while neglecting the financial "big picture" over the long term.

   Financial managers often move into CEO positions. The inventors/innovators of the industry must submit worthy proposals to these financial "wunderkinds." They must prove not if the product or process is worthy, but if the numbers work for the next quarter's printout. While Deming speaks in these exaggerated absolutes, it is clear goals need to be reversed. The financial experts need to discover ways to make things possible for research and development, improvements and the long-term financial well being of the company.

3. **Evaluation by performance, merit rating or annual review of performance.** Deming believes these measurements have the opposite impact on morale and productivity for both managers and workers. They promote fear, inequities, internal competition, anger and discouragement.

4. **Mobility of management.** Managers change jobs because they become discouraged with the companies for whom they work. Because managers are not developed with the "big picture" in mind, they become disenchanted with what they are trying to  accomplish. The organization loses its historical memory and the talent once hired to create its future.

5. **Running a company on visible figures alone.** Deming explains some of the most important figures for a company are "unknowable." They include the multiplier effect of a happy or unhappy customer, the absence of that "extra

mile" by motivated managers and workers that makes all the difference and the hours saved in front-end planning and communicating.

6. **Excessive medical costs for employee health care which increase the final costs of goods and services.** Companies have documented big savings in insurance premiums when prevention takes a front seat in employee health care. Wellness programs, smoking-cessation clinics, health club memberships and regular medical check-ups are frequently cited in studies demonstrating how companies have saved money through the introduction of various health initiatives for employees.

7. **Excessive costs of warranty, fueled by lawyers who work on the basis of contingency fees.** Companies that commit to quality and error-free work realize savings during a warranty period because of very few non-anticipated services. Quality requires companies to get out in front of customer needs and to understand and diminish variance through continuous improvement. Good customer relationships at every point in the process assure a partnership approach. Keeping costs down and delivering services that customers value at a price they are willing to pay are the rewards for doing business by listening to the customer.

## DEMING'S OBSTACLES
Companies may use these obstacles to reject a TQM process.

- **"Hope for instant pudding."** Deming cautions against those who believe improvement of quality and productivity are achieved suddenly by affirmation of faith. The transformation Deming speaks of is a deliberate and time-intensive process and will most likely require a shift in culture — the essence of a company's values, principles and goals. There is no "quick fix."

- **"The supposition that solving problems, automation, gadgets and new machinery will transform industry."** Not by technology alone will organizations achieve their goals. Commitment to develop the new workforce, to listen to the evolving needs of customers and to maintain dependable relationships with suppliers and distributors begin to capture the human side of enterprise. The future includes high-tech as well as high-touch.

- **"Search for examples."** Companies that look for a "roadmap" to follow instead of planning their own route to quality will be disappointed. One company's process cannot be superimposed on another organization. However, it is very beneficial for companies to talk with others who are pretty far along the TQM curve to listen to what they have learned.

- **"Our problems are different."** Managers may reject the experiences of other companies as not relevant to their own. While solutions need to be individualized for each organization, the problems and discoveries of others can provide encouragement and useful insights.

- **"Our quality control department takes care of all our problems of quality."** Stated simply, quality cannot be "assigned" to a department. Total quality is a process, not a program. To achieve total quality, everyone needs to participate in a daily process with deliberation and innovation.

- **"We installed quality control."** There is no end to total quality. It is a way of life where individuals make daily commitments to continuous improvement and cross-functional teams work tenaciously to get incremental results. Total quality is not a light bulb that is turned on and off. Think of it as a whole powerhouse that energizes an entire company.

• **"The supposition that it is necessary only to meet specifications."** Strict compliance will guarantee only keeping up with yesterday's standard. To move into the future, one must recognize that the **"supposition that all is right inside the specifications and all is wrong outside the specifications"** is a fallacy.

## JOSEPH M. JURAN

Joseph Juran (1904 -    ) may be closest to Deming in his approach to quality. They differ on how difficult it is for a company to achieve quality, how important statistical methods are and whether competition is good or bad. Deming believes achieving quality requires "transformation" and a change in organizational culture; Juran believes an organization can manage for quality.

The Juran Trilogy, a trademark of the Juran Institute, Inc., identifies three areas for quality conversion within a company:

• financial planning becomes quality planning
• financial control becomes quality control
• financial improvement becomes quality improvement

Juran is credited as the first person to attempt to measure the cost of quality. He successfully demonstrated to management what potential increases in profit would occur if the costs of poor quality were lowered. (Feigenbaum further advanced this reasoning with the "cost of non-conformance" argument.)

Juran does not believe managing for quality is as easy as Phil Crosby thinks it is, but certainly not as difficult as Deming believes it to be. He does concede most quality programs fail because companies do not understand how difficult it is going to be to develop new processes. Still, Juran believes quality, like finance, can be managed.

Juran is less impressed with statistics than Deming. Juran views statistical methods as a tool and understands both their merits and limitations. He believes quality starts with knowing who the customers are and what the customers need. Producing goods and services targeted to the right niche markets using the most appropriate technology is no easy accomplishment. Juran agrees that management's commitment to customers, suppliers and employees are at the core of quality. His definition of quality has expanded over the years since his first visit to post-war Japan. He defines quality as "fitness for use," including product/service features desired by the customers and assured "freedom from failure."

When Juran made his first visit to Japan in 1954 after the publication of his *Quality Control Handbook* (1951), the Japanese were trained extensively in statistical methods. They wanted to understand management's role in quality. The Japanese Union of Scientists and Engineers (JUSE) invited Juran to teach them management's responsibilities. In *Out of Crisis* (1986), Deming praised Juran for his work: "His masterful teaching gave Japanese management new insight into management's responsibility for improvement of quality and productivity."

Juran points to three imperatives for total quality to take hold in a company:

- commitment and action from top management
- training in Total Quality Management
- quality improvements at an unprecedented rate

Quality has improved in the United States, but not at a rate comparable to Japan. Juran speaks about a need for a "revolutionary rate of improvement." It is true that Juran and Deming's ideas are very close indeed. The global marketplace is setting new standards in excellence in both products and processes, both of which result in lower costs for the customer.

In 1981, Juran was honored by the Japanese with the award of the Second Order Medal, just as Deming had been recognized in 1960. As a credit to Juran's impact, Japan has more information on quality control than any other nation. JUSE published 660 books on quality control between 1960 and 1985. In 1987, Tokyo University offered 520 courses in Total Quality Control (TQC) for 48,560 students. Juran has developed a series of videotapes, "Juran on Quality," which are available through the Juran Institute in Wilton, Connecticut. Founded by Juran in 1979, the institute's leadership was transferred in 1987 to Blanton Godfrey, a former AT&T executive. Juran still consults and advises at the institute.

---

**JURAN'S 10 STEPS TO QUALITY IMPROVEMENT: DIRECTIVES FOR MANAGEMENT**

1. Build awareness for the need and opportunity for improvement.

2. Set goals for improvement.

3. Organize to reach the goals. For example, establish a quality council, identify problems, select processes which need improvement, appoint teams, train facilitators and team members.

4. Provide training throughout the organization.

5. Carry out projects to solve problems.

6. Report progress.

7. Give recognition.

8. Communicate results.

9. Keep score.

10. Maintain momentum by making annual improvement part of the regular systems and processes of the company.

Joseph M. Juran, ed.
*Quality Control Handbook*
McGraw-Hill, 1951

---

## ARMAND FEIGENBAUM

Armand Feigenbaum (1920 -   ) founded General Systems in Pittsfield, Mass., in 1968. He is credited with grabbing the attention of corporate leaders by advancing the "cost of nonconformance" approach as a rationale for a commitment to quality. He elevated the importance of expenditures for initiatives that achieve higher quality by demonstrating geometric return on investment (ROI). Further, he has made the argument that those companies practicing Total Quality Management are setting the international standards for quality in their industries.

At 24, Feigenbaum was General Electric's (GE) top quality expert. He understood that the achievement of quality is the result of a total orchestration of all inputs. He discovered "quality was not a group of individual techniques or tools; instead, it was a total field." By integrating the planning, implementation and evaluation of processes among various contributors, Feigenbaum achieved higher quality.

In 1961, Feigenbaum's book, *Total Quality Control,* was published. His views on work-process flows began to question the isolation of the earlier quality-assurance methods of sampling and inspection. Feigenbaum realized that whenever he gained improvements on a particular GE process, everything in the organization began to improve.

People were energized by improved systems and methods. They fed on one another's successes because Feigenbaum understood systems theory and created an environment where they could learn from their own experience. His leadership led to cross-functional teamwork and an open work environment, which provided some of the footprints for focus groups and improvement teams.

Feigenbaum believes the customer defines quality. Deming disagrees to some extent. Deming advises that the real edge comes to the companies who learn their customers so well that they can anticipate their future needs. The companies that are not in touch with those needs simply will not stay in business.

Feigenbaum offers convincing proof of his view about delivering quality to customers with his point on the cost of nonconformance. In a 1988 General Systems' consumer and industrial markets survey, eight out of 10 buyers put quality ahead of price in their decision to buy. In 1979, it was three out of 10.

Feigenbaum is a staunch advocate of the American worker.

Having traveled and worked in numerous countries around the world, he affirms that the American worker has no equal "when given full and necessary support and leadership from management." Feigenbaum is very optimistic that U.S. companies will achieve expansive results with TQM, as long as management is committed to the heart of the matter — customers, suppliers and employees.

Feigenbaum identified 40 steps to quality improvement. Listed below are the six key steps:

## ARMAND FEIGENBAUM'S KEY POINTS

1. Total quality control may be defined as an effective system for integrating the quality-development, quality-maintenance and quality-improvement efforts of the various groups in an organization so as to enable marketing, engineering, production and service at the most economical levels which allow for full customer satisfaction.

2. In the phrase "quality control," the word control represents a management tool with four steps:

   a. setting quality standards
   b. appraising performance to these standards
   c. acting when the standards are exceeded
   d. planning for improvement in the standards

3. The factors affecting product quality can be divided into two major groupings:

   a. the technological (including processes)
   b. the human

   Of these two factors, the human is of greater importance by far.

4. Quality control enters into all phases of the industrial production process, starting with the industrial customer's

specification and the sale to the customer, through design, engineering and assembly, to shipment of the product and installation and field service for a customer who remains satisfied with the product.

5. Operating quality costs are divided into four different classifications:

   a. **prevention costs**, which include quality planning and other costs associated with preventing nonconformance and defects

   b. **appraisal costs**, or the costs incurred in evaluating product quality to maintain established standards

   c. **internal failure costs**, caused by defective and nonconforming materials and products that do not meet the company quality specifications. These include scrap, rework and spoilage

   d. **external failure costs**, caused by the defective and nonconforming products reaching the customer. They include complaints and warranty product service costs, costs of product recall, court costs and liability penalties.

   (**NOTE**: External failure costs also include loss of repeat business — one of Deming's "unknowable" numbers — and loss of market share.)

6. An important feature of a total quality program is that it controls quality at the source. An example is its positive effect in stimulating and building up operator responsibility for and interest in product quality through measurements taken by the operator at the station.

A.V. Feigenbaum
*Total Quality Control*
McGraw-Hill, 1961

# PHILIP CROSBY

Phil Crosby (1926 -    ), the first U.S. corporate vice president for quality at ITT in the 1970s, is recognized as the guru who brought Total Quality to the boardroom and off the shop floor. He is pragmatic, straightforward and translates complex concepts into language business people understand.

Crosby's *Quality is Free*, published in 1979, has sold more than two million copies and is available in several languages. In it, he quotes then-ITT chairman Harold S. Geneen:

> "Quality is not only right,  it is free. And it is not only free, it is the most profitable product line we have."

Crosby created the zero-defect movement at Martin Marietta in the 1960s. He popularized the slogan "do it right the first time," which was first used at Western Electric in the mid-30s.

After working in quality control and assurance for a number of years and studying Deming and Juran, Crosby was frustrated with the ongoing existence of defects. He disagrees with Deming and believes zero defects can be achieved.

Crosby began to focus on prevention. He pressed management about why they accepted the statistical theory that a few things will always be bad. He argued that "it must be cheaper to do things right the first time." Management at Martin Marietta needed to hear this logic. Given the critical nature of the company's work with the government in delivering very precise and complex military technology, Crosby's viewpoint placed him front and center on the quality stage.

Crosby operates Philip Crosby Associates, Inc., with a staff of 325 people located in six states, as well as in London, Paris, Munich, Genoa, Toronto, Singapore, Sydney and Tokyo. In contrast, Deming has had one staff person, Cecelia Kilian, who began working with him in the basement office of his Washington D.C. home in 1954.

Crosby has worked with more than 1,500 companies. People attend his schools to learn about his 14-Point Program — of which there are four basics he calls the Absolutes of Quality Management. They are listed on the following pages.

Crosby's approach is pragmatic and energetic. He is alone among all the quality experts in believing that achieving quality can be relatively easy. Crosby is an excellent presenter. He has been credited with providing a clear voice and a distinct message on quality that U.S. business is finally coming to understand. Deming faults Crosby for oversimplifying what is really necessary for companies to do in order to achieve TQM. They do agree, as do the rest of the experts, that statistical analysis is a very small part of the whole. The emphasis is on people.

## CROSBY'S FOUR ABSOLUTES OF QUALITY MANAGEMENT

1. **The definition of quality is conformance to requirements.** Frequently, this is misunderstood to mean conformance to specifications. Crosby believes the final product or service in a TQM environment reflects a 10 percent conformance to specifications and a 90 percent response to what the customer wants.

2. **The system of causing quality is prevention.** In order to reduce costs, inspection needs to be eliminated. In a TQM organization, the system itself must produce quality on its own. The implications for developing employees to understand the whole job and troubleshoot the system for improvements at every stage is clear.

3. **The performance standard for quality is zero defects.** Crosby believes statistical laws are fabrications that promote the myth that defects are inevitable. He simply believes companies can perform at a zero-defect rate. None of the other experts believe this is even a possibility.

4. **The measurement of quality is the price of nonconformance.** Crosby added on to the work Feigenbaum had done at GE and demonstrated with hard numbers that it costs

more not to produce quality than it does to produce it. The experience of TQM companies holds this absolute to be true.

## CROSBY'S 14 POINTS

1. **Management commitment.** To make it clear where management stands on quality, Crosby challenges management to provide focus and strategy and to center its quality efforts on the needs of customers.

2. **Quality improvement team.** The quality improvement process is continuous and so are the improvements in maintaining a quality edge.

3. **Measurement.** To provide a display of current and potential nonconformance problems in a manner that permits objective evaluation and corrective action. A company needs to understand its baseline and commit to controlling variance.

4. **Cost of quality.** To define the ingredients of the Cost of Quality (COQ) and explain its use as a management tool. The real COQ problems arise when the company is not focused on quality methods and results.

5. **Quality awareness.** To provide a method of raising the personal concern felt by all employees toward the conformance of the product or service and the quality reputation of the company. Training in TQM principles and practices is key.

6. **Corrective action.** To provide a systematic method of resolving forever the problems that are identified through the previous action steps. Quality at the source empowers people to intervene at any step of the process.

7., 9. **Zero-defects planning and zero-defects day.** To examine the various activities that must be conducted in preparation for formally launching a zero-defects day. To create an event that will let all employees realize, through a personal experience, that there has been a change.

8. **Employee education.** To define the type of training all employees need in order to actively carry out their roles in the quality-improvement process. Pilot programs provide a viable way for organizations to introduce an integrated process from which "new learning" is captured and translated to other parts of the company.

10. **Goal setting.** To turn pledges and commitments into action by encouraging individuals to establish improvement goals for themselves and their groups. Setting targets brings people together to work toward the same end.

11. **Error cause removal.** To give the individual employee a method of communicating to management the situations that make it difficult for the employee to meet the pledge to improve. Crosby is clear that management needs to understand the experience of its workers to provide supportive work environments structured to deliver the results it wants.

12. **Recognition.** To appreciate those who participate. People need recognition for their efforts. Managers report that it is the "simple thank you" which makes the difference.

13. **Quality councils.** To bring together the appropriate people to share quality-management information on a regular basis. Councils are one way to keep quality and its benefits at the forefront of running companies.

14. **Do it all over again.** To emphasize that the quality-improvement process is continuous. Quality is never

thought of as a project with a beginning, middle and end. Quality requires a dynamic process that is responsive to new requirements and standards.

## KAORU ISHIKAWA

Kaoru Ishikawa, who died in 1989, graduated from Tokyo University in 1938 and is probably the best known of the Japanese quality gurus. His father, Ichiro Ishikawa, as president of the Japanese Union of Science and Engineering (JUSE) and the Federation of Economic Organizations, encouraged the Japanese to accept the message brought to them by Deming and Juran. He died in 1970.

In 1949, Ishikawa was already talking about statistical methods of quality control to the Japanese. Americans visited Japan in the early 1970s to learn about quality-control circles and the impact they were having on productivity. It was Ishikawa who began them in 1962. He was very successful in enlisting senior Japanese management to listen to the suggestions that came out of the quality circles (QCs) and in allowing the QCs their autonomy to solve problems.

American managers liked the idea of quality circles because they shifted responsibility to American workers. However, American senior management never actually trusted them enough to allow their full impact. When the Americans observed QCs in Japan, they really did not understand where they fit in the company structure. Crosby explains that since QCs are more a process than a form and because Americans couldn't actually "see" them in a Japanese organization, they really didn't know how to import them to the United States.

Ishikawa credits Deming with introducing quality control to Japan in 1950 and also recognizes the contributions of both Shewhart and Juran. Initially Ishikawa believed there was too much emphasis on statistical methods, but he was very encouraged after Juran's visit in 1954, which focused on management processes and identified quality control as a management tool. In *What Is Total Quality Control?* Ishikawa credits Feigenbaum with the concept of total quality control (TQC). However, Ishikawa believes that Feigenbaum was misguided when he placed TQC in the quality-control department and with quality-control specialists. Ishikawa presented the following evidence of his view of organizations and the contributions he expects workers to make.

> "Since 1949, we have insisted on having all divisions and all employees become involved in studying and promoting QC."

Crosby and Ishikawa agree on some of the basics. Top management needs to provide continuous support and leadership and to serve as a role model for employees in their commitment to quality. Top management needs to set standards and measure individual and group initiative and results in these broad areas. Top management has the main responsibility for poor quality. Both men agree quality improvement will reduce costs. Crosby wants to show management the cost of not producing quality; Ishikawa wants to show everyone.

Ishikawa defines the customer as whoever gets the work next. He was the first quality expert to actually focus on internal as well as external customers. He understood process and the fact that process flowed through people. From the beginning and more than anyone, he formed the notion of a shared vision that unifies all people in an organization around that vision and its mission and goal. Ishikawa exemplifies this belief in another statement.

> "Company-wide quality control cannot be complete without total acceptance of this kind of approach by all workers. Sectionalism has to be broken down, and the company has to be ventilated so that everyone can enjoy a breath of fresh air."

Ishikawa was recognized for his unique contributions in quality when he was awarded the Deming Prize in 1952.

## GENICHI TAGUCHI

Genichi Taguchi is best known for the Taguchi Loss Function, which has roots in some of Deming's teachings and which Crosby believes would be hard to apply in most American companies. The Loss Function demonstrates a formula to determine the cost of a lack of quality. Deming, on the other hand, believes it is impossible to calculate the actual cost of the loss of quality. Taguchi, however, is very serious about the validity of his Loss Function.

His principle states that for each deviation there is an incremental economic loss of some geometric proportion. The cumulative impact can be very great if a number of parts are off by just a little. Taguchi's belief is the opposite of the traditional view that states there will be no detrimental impact as long as the parts are within the engineering tolerances or specifications. Therefore, designing to specifications when many parts are at the further end of those tolerances can have an overall negative impact on quality and profit.

**The Taguchi Loss Function**

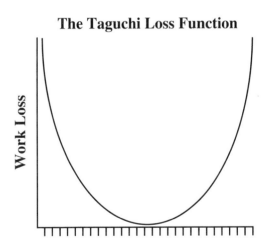

The practical application of the Taguchi Loss Control Function can save a company a lot of money. This method was applied to a car transmission made by the Ford Motor Company. Its warranty losses were corrected because Ford was able to achieve less variation and therefore greater quality.

You can think of this concept in terms of the management of a company. Consider the interrelationships and interdependence among finance, marketing, sales and information systems. Each group has systems and procedures it has developed to achieve its goals. In order for each department to perform optimally, all work from the other departments must be understood and incorporated into a flow chart. This way the integrity of the whole is learned and adhered to.

Following Taguchi's thinking, if all systems and schedules are off slightly there may be little impact per individual event in its own department. Taken collectively, the toll will be far greater. If each department missed a deadline by a day or two, the total impact will have greater consequences for the end customer in the chain.

Preventive steps demand up-front planning and flow charting by managers and employees to gain a full understanding of goals and responsibilities. Anticipating how the batons are passed, benchmarking and identifying contingency plans are just a few things that Taguchi recommends. Cross-functional teams and on-line systems coupled with regular face-to-face communication among all the parties involved are also critical.

Taguchi, like Ishikawa before him, was awarded the Deming Prize in 1960.

## STATISTICAL CHARTS

The charts included in this handbook have evolved from the quality movement over the years. They are simple graphic representations of underlying processes that track variation and guide people to think in logical ways.

Before examining the Seven Basic Tools included in this section, compare step-function change to continuous improvement. Step-function change represents those events which are planned and methodical. Improvements are sequential, logical and create improvement over time. A system will operate in a state of equilibrium until the next planned change occurs, and the system picks up and propels itself to the next rung. There it rests on a plateau until next time.

In contrast, change along the continuous-improvement chart is less predictable and occurs in smaller increments. However, change and improvement are constants. Over time, the gains made are greater than in step-function. There is more fluidity and energy in the continuous-improvement method because all people in the process-flow change are driving the improvements.

The Seven Basic Tools Charts are accompanied by brief descriptions. Note the large representation of the Ishikawa fishbone diagram (cause and effect), as well as the combination of the process-flow analysis and improvement chart. The charts represent logical thought processes and provide a way to analyze systems and events.

The process-flow analysis and improvement-chart layers offer reflections on the cause and effect of certain variables. Diagramming provides insights that our thought patterns — left undiagrammed — might take longer to discover.

## THE SEVEN BASIC TOOLS FOR TQM

1. **Cause-and-effect diagrams** are also known as fishbone diagrams because of their shape and as Ishikawa diagrams because of their originator. They are typically used to depict causes of certain problems and to group them according to categories, such as method, manpower, material and machinery.

2. **Flow charts or process-flow diagrams** are the visual representation of the steps in a process. They are particularly useful in the service industries, where work involves unseen steps.

3. **Pareto charts are simple bar charts** used after data collection to rank causes so that priorities can be assigned. Their use gives rise to the 80-20 Rule — that 80 percent of the problems stem from 20 percent of the causes.

4. **Run (trend) charts** simply show the results of a process plotted over a period of time. For example, it can show sales per month.

5. **Histograms** are used to measure the frequency with which something occurs. For example, it measures how often a train departs 10 minutes late as opposed to five minutes or 60 minutes.

6. **Scatter diagrams** illustrate the relationship between two variables, such as height and weight. As points for events are plotted, relationships can be determined and similar clusters and deviations can be observed.

7. **Control charts** are the most advanced of the seven basic tools and are used to reflect variation in a system. They are run charts with statistically determined upper and lower limits. As long as the process variables fall within the range, the system is said to be "in control" and its variation to stem from a common cause. The goal is to narrow the range between the upper and lower limits by seeking to eliminate the common causes that occur day in and day out. Controlling variation equates to controlling cost and conforming to requirements.

# SEVEN BASIC TOOLS CHARTS

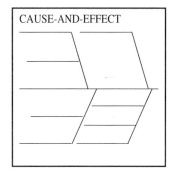

CAUSE-AND-EFFECT

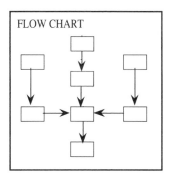

FLOW CHART

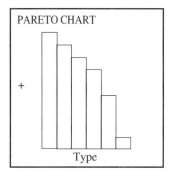

PARETO CHART

Type

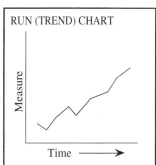

RUN (TREND) CHART

Measure

Time

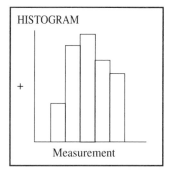

HISTOGRAM

Measurement

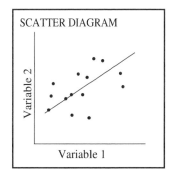

SCATTER DIAGRAM

Variable 2

Variable 1

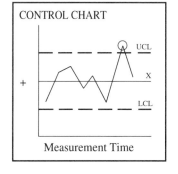

CONTROL CHART

UCL

X

LCL

Measurement Time

# PROCESS FLOW

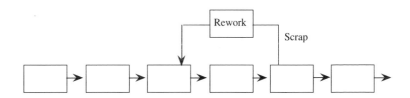

# CAUSE-AND-EFFECT DIAGRAM
## (Ishikawa Fishbone Diagram)

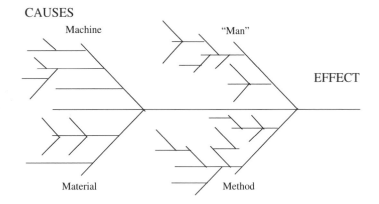

# PROCESS-FLOW ANALYSIS AND IMPROVEMENT

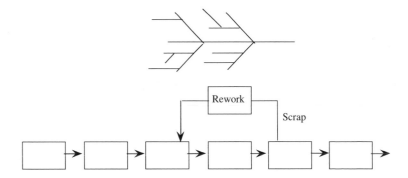

# 4

## CURRENT STATE OF THE QUALITY MOVEMENT

### MALCOLM BALDRIDGE NATIONAL QUALITY AWARD
### KEY POINTS FOR EVALUATION

Many American companies use criteria from the Malcolm Baldridge National Quality Award to strengthen their own quality-management processes. Named for the former Secretary of Commerce, the award was established by an Act of Congress in 1987 to:

- promote quality awareness
- recognize quality achievements of U.S. companies
- publicize successful quality strategies

The following criteria outline areas in which companies compete to demonstrate their performance excellence in quality.

## LEADERSHIP
- Senior management involvement
- Quality values
- Management system
- Public responsibility

## INFORMATION ANALYSIS
- Scope of information and data
- Data management
- Analysis and use of data

## STRATEGIC QUALITY PLANNING
- Planning process
- Plans for quality leadership benchmarking
- Priorities

## HUMAN RESOURCE UTILIZATION
- Management
- Employee involvement
- Education and training
- Employee recognition
- Quality of worklife

## QUALITY ASSURANCE
- Design and introduction of products and services
- Operation of processes
- Measurements and standards
- Audit
- Documentation

• Business processes
• External providers of goods and services

## QUALITY RESULTS
• Quality of products and services
• Competitive comparison
• Operational and business process quality improvement
• Supplier quality improvement

## CUSTOMER SATISFACTION
• Knowledge of customer requirements and expectations
• Customer-relationship management
• Commitment
• Complaint management
• Customer-satisfaction determination
• Customer-satisfaction trends

## FOR MORE INFORMATION ABOUT THE BALDRIDGE AWARD:

**Malcolm Baldridge National Quality Award**
National Institute of Standards and Technology
Administration Building, Room A537
Gaithersburg, MD  20899

**Telephone:** (301) 975-2036
**FAX:** (301) 948-3716

## TQM READINESS AND ORGANIZATIONAL IMPACT
Companies and managers eager to improve quality and productivity are hungry for the results that TQM can deliver. These companies frequently ask, "Where do we start?" The first step is one of the most difficult. Stand still and assess the organization or

your division or department as it exists and functions today. You should take time to review the TQM Readiness Quiz detailed in this section with your co-workers. The examples describe many real work situations that will give you insight on how TQM works and how far along your organization is in the process.

Consultants experienced in working with TQM companies and in designing organization and management assessments can provide clear methodology in assessing your company's position. A recommended, external team can assess the TQM readiness of your company through an assessment tool. Feedback from surveys, structured interviews and focus groups with managers, employees, suppliers and customers can provide a strong base of credible data. This data is systematically collected and reported.

## THE McKINSEY 7-S MODEL

The McKinsey 7-S Model, shown on the next page, demonstrates that TQM is both a philosophy and a way of doing things which threads all of the components of the 7-S Model together. An organization's, division's or department's strategy, structure and style of management, as well as its shared values, systems, staffing and the skills and expertise of its human resources all have to be aligned around the driving principles of TQM:

- customer service and satisfaction
- high employee participation
- elimination of waste
- continuous improvement
- higher quality at lower cost

## The 7-S Method

## CULTURE CHANGE AND SHIFTING PARADIGMS

Companies that have embraced TQM report not only is work processed differently, but people at work think and feel differently. The culture change that accompanies implementation of a Total Quality Process creates greater employee participation in identifying and solving problems, in establishing baseline performance standards and in measuring for continuous improvements. Employees delight in making better products that save both the company and customers money while adding greater value.

Employees report there is a renewal of collaboration and a stronger work ethic. People become energized around achieving goals and targets which they monitor and advance. Structures are flatter, people participate more directly in decision-making, and they are recognized and rewarded for making improvements and for team approaches to problem-solving.

In this section, you will note several descriptions of how companies are working in different ways in a TQM environment. The analysis demonstrates shifting paradigms — a description of a pattern of behavior that reflects a definite change from how things used to be thought of and understood and from how things were done. The examples in the TQM Readiness Quiz show a "before" and "after" snapshot of the impact of TQM.

Also refer to the following profiles, which demonstrate how TQM creates change within companies:

- TQM and management focus
- TQM and attitude change
- TQM and culture change
- TQM and company responsiveness

## TQM READINESS ASSESSMENT

Using the McKinsey 7-S framework, review the accompanying descriptions to see how far along the TQM curve your company, division or department may be. Note the next points to reach. To take the following assessment, circle the statement which best reflects the atmosphere of your current situation. The more fives the better. Discuss these scenarios with people at your company to determine how effective your company is in practicing TQM.

## A. TQM Principles Linked with Business and Market Strategy

1. Only a few people in top management talk about quality as important to our success with our customers.

2. There is a sign in our lobby which says, "Quality is our only business." But our performance is based on getting things done on time to meet budget. We still check things later instead of troubleshooting them along the way. We deal with customers only when they complain. Ultimately, we lose even more money in rework.

3. There was something that the company did a while ago to tell a lot of the employees about how important quality is for our competitiveness. The president talked to us in small

groups and showed us a film. I liked the part about giving employees more responsibility to drive their own improvements geared toward customer requirements. But there hasn't been anything else in six months — no training or new work assignments.

4. We have all gone through 20 hours of training in TQM principles, and soon we start a class in group problem-solving skills. The class will "troubleshoot" factors that influenced my client's decision to leave the company because we couldn't modify our design fast enough to compete with a new product offered by one of our newest competitors. We are going to do a root-cause analysis of the situation to discover ways we might have been more responsive sooner.

5. I am excited because I am on a new product-development team with people from different parts of the company, including several customers and suppliers. Our idea won an award for innovation, and we have been funded to create it. This is such a different place to work than my last company. You know, I submitted that idea to my old boss. He liked ideas on paper with lots of charts, but he never even talked about it with me and looked puzzled one day when I asked him for a response.

## B. Structure and TQM Flex

1. Our company is still very traditional. If I need a report from my counterpart in finance, I have to ask my boss to ask my colleague's boss to send it to me. It may take 10 days before I get it. But I found a short cut through Management of Information Systems, and that takes only five business days. Actually, I spend a good part of my time on the job figuring out how to get around all the hierarchy. There are lots of egos here.

2. Our division just exchanged vice presidents with research and development for a few months. I guess it's a good idea. The marketing VP wanted to learn more about what happens in R&D, and the VP of R&D wanted to get a better sense of marketing and client development. He just wanted to meet some of the customers. I wonder what impact that will have on my work. It's exciting, but I'm nervous I won't be much help.

3. My boss asked me to sit in on a meeting the "big guys" had the other day with one of our primary clients. Even though I wasn't supposed to ask questions, I learned a lot. Meeting the customer and listening to what they think their problems are will help a great deal when I do the rework on their project.

4. I have just been appointed group leader to conduct some benchmarking for a product-review process. There are people on the team from finance, engineering, research and development, marketing, purchasing and manufacturing. Our job is to create our own product-review process aimed at eliminating waste, reducing cost and improving quality.

5. Our new department manager is really making waves. Top management gave her full command of the bonuses for our group for the year. Instead of rewarding the two stars who usually get all the money every year anyway because they have "cracked" the system and because of their buddies inside and outside the company who really give them an edge, everyone in the department will get a chance to earn his share. That new manager is very smart. She has put new incentives in the mix that really speak to the needs of the customers, and reward both individuals and the team for strong performance above the baseline. We set that ourselves last fall when she came. If it works, I think we can bottle it!

## C. Management Style

1. Most everything at my company is top down. We just wait for the word before we do anything. Those of us that have tried to go forward with our own ideas find out sooner or later that management doesn't want any. There is no encouragement to be creative. In fact, the opposite is true — people are penalized for initiative.

2. Even though we never interact with the president, our division heads explain that they are asked what they think about things. Recently, the president has asked his managers to make better presentations describing and analyzing issues related to customer satisfaction. Still, the word is that the president doesn't take his head honchos seriously enough, and these guys, in turn, don't really ask us to contribute much. It's a beginning, but more needs to happen in order for this company to really benefit from its employees.

3. Something's up. My boss recently asked me to review her management style. She said that her division head is asking all his managers to get feedback from their employees. The division head has been here only three months. My boss said they want to make a point to top management, who play most cards close to their vests — that people throughout the company need management training to help them take more initiative. The division head believes the company needs to train and support employee participation and performance. The company has conducted optional sessions for employees to learn how to communicate better, but very few people have participated — mostly because management isn't involved. Basically, employees don't want to feel it's "their" problem. Maybe the new division head will make some headway in showing top management that communication and performance problems start at the top. Still, they are like a lone soldier in this mission. I am glad my boss is supporting them.

4. Our new president tells us he is committed to good management practices. But there are some real inconsistencies. People respect the president of the company, who really is a technical genius in his field. We think he is learning his new role. The president has an open-door policy on communication. Every two weeks he has a meeting with a group of six to eight employees from throughout the company — just to listen to their ideas and concerns. Recently, as part of the evaluation of senior managers' performance, the president added an assessment of their active efforts to develop their employees. On the other hand, a recommendation to have our first customers' user conference was put on hold. We are not sure why. Some say the president is hesitant to have such a face-to-face with customers. He is sincere, but maybe he just needs time and development of his own. Meanwhile, some really good senior managers here are frustrated.

5. Our company has instituted its own management-development program with a leading university. People selected for the program are expected to encourage their employees to assess their management style and to create a work environment that reflects the values and goals of the company. Managers who have gone through the program are also expected to have action plans to help them translate new learning into real-world job applications. The departments that have sent people through the program are achieving higher employee participation and are beginning to have a recognized impact on the bottom line.

## D.   Shared Values

1. There is very little discussion or visible representation at my company of its values. Yet, we definitely have a culture at work here. It is internally competitive. People are guarded, and everyone passes the buck. No one is responsible for anything here, and the last person anyone

wants to hear from is a customer. Customers are looked at as an interference in getting a day's work done. The same is true for other employees who are our internal customers. The expectation is to get things done as quickly and quietly as possible and move the work along to the next point. Quality is rarely discussed.

2. The company recently placed a quality statement in the lobby and distributed it to all departments. I think this is the first time I have heard anything overt here about what our company stands for. The words are great — commitment to customers and employees in developing the highest quality products and services — but much remains to be seen. We have some real morale problems because top management has been out of touch. Our company has gone through a merger in the past five years, and we acquired another company. Our resources are stressed, and, due to the company's poor market performance last year, we are losing 2,700 workers in the U.S. this year. Still, salaries and bonuses for top management saw a 12-percent increase this year. That's irresponsible and speaks louder than any quality statement in our lobby.

3. We have a customer-service policy that reflects the values of the company. Customers are our first priority, and their complaints and recommendations are taken seriously. Most employees practice this out of their own good conscientious service. But employees are not always treated with respect. Managers frequently undermine supervisors, and supervisors pass that behavior along to employees. It is still a top-down company where the individual employee is the last one considered to have a valid opinion. Our employees take pride in our work, but we need to feel better about the values of the company.

4. My boss recently asked us to work on a values statement for our department. Even though one doesn't exist for the

company, they thought we could create one for our department. My boss says top management is focused on strategy for the company and sometimes takes the internal operation and work environment for granted. My boss believes managers and supervisors can help shape the culture of the company. They can initiate ideas and practices at different levels and find ways to integrate these in other departments. My boss is very effective, and I believe what he says. Our communication in our department is straightforward and clear. We always know where we stand with each other and collaborate to get the job done. I credit our boss because he really knows how to treat people fairly. He also has the respect and the ear of top management.

5. Our company practices what it preaches. Top management has a lot of integrity and knows how to treat employees with respect. The demands are very great on our performance and productivity, but it is obvious top management is up to the challenge and so are we. Communication is excellent. Training is a norm, and policies and practices are geared toward customer service and satisfaction and continuous improvement. We practice winning at the company, and anyone who wants to "play the game for real" will succeed here.

## E.   Systems

1. Our company is not efficiently organized, and employees do not receive orientation on the practices and systems of other departments. Each division and department keeps its own records and has its own systems. Each one feeds the results of its work to the top, where it is somehow integrated. But none of us is ever really sure where we are in relation to the whole. We even have different grade levels and compensation packages among the divisions. There are no uniform programs for personal computer

users. There are different performance-review practices, varying amounts delegated to training and research and development and diverse ways divisions and departments are organized. People don't have a clear understanding of how work flows through the system. We waste time trying to clear up the confusion on our own.

2. The company has a rigid system for processing work. It is very precise, and each step is checked by three levels of management. The company has been committed to quality for a long time and takes a painstaking approach to guarantee that standards and procedures are met. Employees complain that there is a little too much "automatic pilot." They feel there is not room to innovate or create process improvements to achieve better efficiency and reduce costs. Management is dubious of loosening some of its rigid methods; they need to learn to trust employees.

3. The company has just announced it will begin benchmarking a new research process for developing innovative products. We are excited about this because at last year's annual employees' meeting, this was the number-one suggestion to improve our market performance. Employees believed their productivity was high, but the company was falling behind in adapting to new demands from the marketplace. Competitors were gaining ground because they were better at coming out with products that were targeted to specific market segments. Employees feel acknowledged for their input, but are waiting to hear from top management about what their roles will be. In the past, the company has operated in a linear manner — one foot after another.

4. My boss asked me to attend a one-week course in product review. He wants me to discover what things might be useful for our department in analyzing product design and

development improvements. This is the first time anyone at the company has asked me to address this issue. I am pleased because I have heard that the new division director wants people to focus on improvements in our products. This shows me we are headed in the right direction in meeting customer requirements and maintaining our commitment to quality products.

5. A few managers have gotten together recently to discuss problems in the breakdown of how work is being processed. We are finding out a lot about how each department gets its job done. We were surprised to learn how often we get in one another's way just to meet our own deadlines. We are uncovering lots of problems which we can correct to make the entire process work better for everyone. We are taking our recommendations to senior management because we need to make some structural and procedural adjustments that will make things work more responsively to our goals. We expect top management to support the recommendations. They usually do and find ways to recognize and reward us for working as a team.

## F. Staffing

1. The company is outdated in how it recruits people. It is still an "old boys" network on top and barely responsive to affirmative action. People are not trained or developed, and the "status quo" is reflected in how people are rewarded for emulating the style at the top.

2. The company takes a very direct role in recruiting people with the highest technical credentials. It is an exciting place to work because there are professionals here from all over the world. However, we need training and development in better management practices. We could also benefit from taking more advantage of our cultural diversity. We could learn more about the preferences of our international

customer base from our own employees. Management is not very active in developing managers or in creating opportunities for these cultural orientations. Division leaders and department managers need to put their heads together to maximize our potential.

3. I have been encouraged by the leadership my department head takes to assist each of us in understanding our jobs and in setting both individual and group goals. He also listens to where we need help and assists us in identifying things which will make us more effective. People in the department know they are being treated as individuals, and performance shows it. Our company does not have a unified approach to its employees, however. Each department's success in hiring and developing employees is as good as the manager in each department.

4. Managers are pulling together in attacking the problem of how to get more done with less. After last year's downsizing, the people that were left have been knocking themselves out just trying to meet goals. Now, management is beginning to see burnout and stress. Supervisors are pleased to see their concerns have resulted in something. Managers are uniting and formalizing their analysis with our input to present to top management. Companies only improve when real issues are tackled. The managers are taking initiative, and they are united. The atmosphere is positive around solving problems. Managers are not blaming anyone, but they want top management's support.

5. Great progress is being made in the management of our human resources. Our company has always been an industry leader in recruitment and training. We have both employee- and customer-feedback surveys, and top management reports back on the progress made within a year to address key concerns. Now we are forging new ground in work arrangements that recognize employees'

individual life circumstances. We have flex time, flex space, where some employees actually work at home and job sharing. The company offers cafeteria benefit plans so people select what they need most. Our workforce is diverse in cultural backgrounds. The company promotes this with different ethnic-awareness days when the cafeteria provides optional ethnic foods. There are noon-time films and discussions on customs and norms of other cultures. Foreign-language classes have been offered for the past two years.

## G. Skills

1. My company seems to have no understanding of what real skills are needed to achieve various jobs. They seem to recruit people who fit in with the culture reflected in the values of our president. Then they think the person will grow into the position. This really frustrates people who are already equipped to get the job done, and it seriously hampers our competitive position. I think our human resources department needs better leadership.

2. The company is clear in setting expectations for skill sets it wants employees to have for certain jobs and areas of responsibility. However, no internal training is provided, and our company recently took back its commitment to reimbursing employees for money spent on training programs. Top management acknowledged the decision was a difficult one, but they determined it was up to committed employees to develop themselves in order to give their best effort to their company.

3. Training is a norm where I work. However, each person must identify training sources on his own. The company will pay for it, but it does not sponsor internal programs and is not active in identifying strong programs to support employees in getting state-of-the-art knowledge and training.

4. Our human resources department has recently instituted a new pilot program to develop a needs assessment of employee training and development to keep up with job requirements. Our company made a commitment last month to identify the skills gaps and to develop programs to train employees. This is the first unified step the company has taken to look at itself as a whole.

5. My company is aggressive in recruiting and developing its people. Only the highest-qualified employees are hired, and our managers are expected to work with individuals on a continuous basis to guarantee they stay current in their fields. We have many opportunities within the company to develop cross-training strategies to improve internal understanding of how work is processed and what adds value to the end-product. It is great to work for a company that understands and rewards its employees for being highly-skilled experts.

## TQM AND MANAGEMENT FOCUS

There are focus points for all levels of management within a TQM environment. Commitment to the customer, continuous improvement, elimination of waste, increased employee participation and high-quality, value-added results are key. Following are attributes needed at all company levels.

## SENIOR TEAM

Vision, commitment, strategic goals, steering group, critical processes, role-modeling, mentoring

## MIDDLE MANAGEMENT TEAM

Mission, improvement goals, improvement teams, process improvement, prioritization of improvement opportunities

## OPERATING TEAMS

Improvement goals, skill enhancement, process improvement, function improvement, involvement teams, problem-solving

## TOTAL QUALITY MANAGEMENT: A PARADIGM SHIFT IN ATTITUDES

| **From:** | **To:** |
|---|---|
| Other people are bad and are to be mistrusted. | Other people are good and deserve a climate of trust. |
| Betrayal and failure are a natural way of life. | Honoring commitments and making relationships work are a natural way of life. |
| Blame others when things go wrong. | Work together to make improvements when things go wrong. |
| Concentrate on telling others how they screwed up. | Concentrate on "catching people doing something right." |
| Life is competitive. Cooperation is the exception. | Life is cooperative. Competition is the exception. |
| Personal success is measured in competitive terms. For me to succeed, you must fail. | Success is measured in cooperative terms. Success equals "earning your trust." |
| Excellence is an idealistic dream. | Though it requires discipline and diligence, excellence is within our reach. |

Excellence takes far too much work.

Once the skills have been mastered, a life based on excellence runs more smoothly.

My identity is with my group, not with the organization.

My identity is tied to the entire organization as well as my own group.

Rewards are fixed.  If you want your share, you have to compete.

Rewards can grow if we cooperate.

## TOTAL QUALITY MANAGEMENT: TQM AS ORGANIZATIONAL CULTURE CHANGE

Living in a TQM environment frequently requires a shift in how things get done within a company. Traditional ways of thinking and doing shift to TQM strategies. Note the shifts below.

| | **TRADITIONAL** | **TQM** |
|---|---|---|
| **Heroes** | Firefighters | Fire preventers |
| | Individual champions | Team champions |
| **Approach** | Intuitive | Analytic |
| | Gut feel | Based on data |
| | Isolated | Interpersonal |
| **Focus** | Turf | Coordination |
| | Individualism | Joint-efforts |

| **Climate** | Blame | Problem-solving |
| | CYA | Working together |

| **Morale** | Defensive | Positive |
| | Fear-driven | Free to create |

## TOTAL QUALITY MANAGEMENT: HOW THE PARADIGM SHIFT AFFECTS THE COMPANY

| **From:** | **To:** |
|---|---|
| Excellent quality is perceived as too expensive. | Excellent quality is understood as the path to lower costs. |
| Worker jobs are strictly defined and limited. | Worker jobs include responsibility for continuous improvement. |
| Worker training is narrowly focused on specific job tasks. | Worker training is broadly focused on analytic skills and problem-solving. |
| There are low work standards and frequent punishment for failure. | There are high work standards, and coaching and training are given to ensure success. |
| Customers are angry with product failures. | Customers are satisfied with high product quality. |
| Customers switch companies often out of frustration. | Customers develop long-term relationships with companies who often have sole-source partnerships with their suppliers. |

## STRATEGIC TOOLS FOR ACHIEVING TQM

Standards of excellence that impact an organization's ability to meet customer requirements need to be established in all areas. People need to become aware of what the expectations are in doing their jobs and to have a clear picture of the entire system.

Key ideas related to leadership, supplier-customer relationships (win-win negotiations), cross-functional teams and benchmarking are presented here as strategies used by TQM companies to improve and learn from and with their customers and suppliers.

## LEADERSHIP

"A ship in harbor is safe, but that is not what ships were made for." Without a driving force at the helm, the company will not have a vision of what it can become. Leaders today are in a pivotal position to help their managers see the world in a new way.

Globalization of the economy and the massive telecommunications network may locate a company's primary market halfway around the globe. If a company leader knows how to squint into the future and dream a dream that has not yet been imagined, that company will likely lead the industry and create new ones.

Much is written about the difference between management and leadership. Clearly, a person manages or measures things and systems; he leads people. Similarly, there has been much research on styles of management and personality types of leaders. The style is not so much the issue as are the values that influence that style. It's important how effective a leader is in applying his style with good judgement, strategy and a sense of humor.

Read Stephen Covey's *Principle Centered Leadership*, or Hunter Lewis' *A Question of Values*. The qualities for good leadership start with core values and belief systems that make it possible for the employees to express themselves and be respected.

Leadership into the next century needs to understand Deming's concept of profound knowledge. Leaders of the new world order will create a corporate community that will open its doors to expansive thinking and learning. They will welcome innovators who truly believe the whole is greater than the sum of its parts.

Leaders need to provide an environment for people to create the future. Leaders need to know how to mentor and to continue learning themselves. Clearly, leaders must turn people loose so they can produce the innovations of tomorrow.

## SUPPLIER-CUSTOMER RELATIONSHIPS

Total Quality Management companies are committed to their customers and expect to form partnerships with suppliers who will adopt strong quality criteria of their own. Lowest bid has come to mean lowest quality, and TQM companies are saying, "No thanks."

The new way of looking at work is as an integrated system where people, material, information and services are in constant transport. Quality at the source puts the full responsibility for the integrity and quality of customer service on each person at every step in the chain.

Differentiating all stakeholders in any system is important to tapping into their knowledge base and seeking their participation. U.S. industry loses millions on waste and rework. Taking the time at the beginning of a relationship to clarify what is the focal concern and who needs to be included is very important.

There are many possible financial arrangements to consider in establishing criteria for a partnership. Understanding one another's cash-flow needs will be important to structure fees in order to support one another in the delivery of the total service to the customer.

There will be many creative strategies developed over the next decade to harness financial user requirements. Following the TQM school of thought, companies will need extensive historic data on everything to understand load variables, user rates and how TQM will begin to make a dent in bringing costs down.

Ultimately, TQM will reduce costs, but only if all providers of the end-customer service become partners in the chain. TQM requires the investment of time and analysis to discover what the pieces are. Controlling the margin of variation is where savings are realized. By engaging customers and suppliers with a total quality-improvement process, companies will discover the difference between value/cost — what it actually took to provide the customer's requirements — and value/price — what the customer is actually willing to pay for value-added features.

Negotiations will take on a new flavor when parties spell out real needs and organize around a common goal — serving the customer both now and in the future. Win-win negotiation methods, advanced by Roger Fisher and William Urey, have demonstrated how to achieve keen collaboration. Learning how to get what you want and discovering how another person gets what he wants as well are very powerful tools at any negotiating table.

## CROSS-FUNCTIONAL TEAMS

Having just experienced 20 years of specialization in MBA education, I am now hearing field reports from careerists who are reflecting with 20/20 vision on those greatly heralded degrees. I hear many of the following complaints.
- You never taught me how to negotiate.
- Why wasn't marketing required?
- So what is personality typing anyway?
- What about Workforce 2000?
- Where can I get a "German for Business" class?
- I've been a "star" in every organization I have ever been in; so just what are cross-functional teams?

Cross-functional teams are composed of individuals who come from areas that are distinctly separate from one another and who are committed to improving a process with a common goal. TQM companies like cross-functional teams because people learn more about other parts of the organization and become more familiar with processes and functions different from their own.

Cross-functional teams serve more than an educational function for their members. Information transmitted in face-to-face meetings has a higher frequency rate of being both understood and acted upon. Cross-functional teams achieve real value through pragmatic teamwork and through developing mutual respect for jobs and employees.


## BENCHMARKING

TQM companies use benchmarking to raise their sights and learn about the bright ideas of others that are related to a process important to them. When a CEO begins to speak about TQM improvements he is making within an organization, there are likely to be several supporters waiting in the wings who have already taken on such a process.

Executives at IBM and Xerox said they would go anywhere in the world and look at any industry to learn who is the "best in the breed" in any given effort or process. Benchmarking is an eye-opener. The philosophers have said that the real sadness of adulthood is that people go indoors. We lose touch with nature. Benchmarking invites everyone "out to play."

TQM companies take the time to learn who is already doing it, and who is doing it better than anybody else. Companies are flattered to be emulated. In the new world of transglobal business, it is difficult to say who your competition will be. However, TQM believes it is healthy to hold up their successes and learn from them.

Companies committed to TQM will benchmark all critical processes and listen to some of the trailblazers who have gone before them. In turn, they will be emulated as well.


## WIN-WIN NEGOTIATING METHODS

Negotiations have a different context in TQM environments. As previously mentioned, even negotiations with suppliers take on the new focus of total customer service and satisfaction. Negotiations with clients are developed in an atmosphere of discovering what value-added elements customers want and which ones they are willing to pay more for. How open companies are during a proposal and bid stage may determine how companies work together, if at all. How eager companies are to find creative ways to help their clients solve their problems and save money will be obvious by their ability to work in an open manner.

## ISO 9000 SERIES

With the continued emergence of a global marketplace, a five-standard system called the International Organization for Standardization (ISO) 9000 Series was developed to serve as a common denominator for quality assurance among all companies abiding by these standards. Worldwide, more than 45 countries have accepted these generic standards in businesses, ranging from service providers to manufacturers. These standards have impact on all phases of a business or company from leadership and design to production and delivery. It requires companies to research and document their standards as well as follow, manage, verify and act on recommendations. The ISO 9000 Series does not specify how to comply with the standards, but gives a general guide on what needs to be done. In fact, many companies have based their TQM systems on the ISO 9000 Series standards.

# 5

## WHAT COMPANIES ARE SAYING ABOUT TQM

**WHAT COMPANIES ARE SAYING ABOUT TQM**

It is not through technology alone that TQM has made its impression on those gauging the industrial prowess of the Japanese over the past 40 plus years, as well as the more recent achievements of American total quality companies. It is precisely the blend of statistical and technical processes along with human-management technology that makes many believe this is a unique time of "interactive" ideologies in history. Today, there is an opportunity to take advantage of many ways of knowing quality and to harness those learnings into integrated, intelligent and global ways of doing things. TQM seems to offer this opportunity.

In TQM, art and science meet and meld. The hard sciences synergize with the social sciences. Through TQM, Deming's concept of "profound knowledge" comes to life as systems thinking is applied to both machines and processes and both organizations and people. East meets West. Right brain-left brain "know how" stimulate each other to create a whole that is greater than the sum of its parts.

Whether you believe as Deming that TQM really represents a holistic approach or if you see TQM like Juran as a means to get control of managing quality in products and services, one thing does appear to be true. TQM works.

Companies run better. Customers remain loyal because they are satisfied with the responsiveness of companies. Companies develop high-performance, cross-functional teams. Institutional learning is captured. Data are collected, analyzed and used to make continuous process improvements. Companies invest in training and measure the value of the training by assessing its impact in the workplace. Suppliers and unions "buy in"; and productivity and quality continue to improve while costs for the customer are lowered.

Some say the homogenous Japanese culture promotes the success of TQM, while the diversity of the U.S. culture makes TQM difficult if not impossible. Certainly, America is now on an irreversible journey to discover the answer to this serious question.

The companies who participate in the Baldridge Award have encouraging reports. They explain TQM is not a "quick fix." There is no recipe or roadmap. A weekend course or a month-long seminar at any of the nation's leading universities will not give you the tool kit you might want. TQM does not come in a box or even on a video cassette.

Total Quality Management provides American companies that have committed to it an opportunity to renew or reinvent their corporation from the inside out. TQM is not a program, a new project or management's latest gimmick. TQM is a process that must be developed by each company. Gauge for yourself the impact of the results reported by a few companies working within TQM environments. You may pick up clues of where you can start or determine if you are on the right track.

## XEROX CORPORATION
## STAMFORD, CT
## BUSINESS PRODUCTS AND SERVICES DIVISION
### 1990 Baldridge Winner

Xerox was losing market share rapidly in the early 1980s. By 1980, the Japanese had 20 percent of the U.S. auto market, but they had 40 percent of the U.S. copier business. Domestic as well as foreign competitors were surpassing Xerox in both the cost and quality of reprographic products. Xerox was in crisis.

In 1984, Xerox launched an ambitious program of "Leadership Through Quality." The company invested $125 million in training over the next five years. Initially every employee received 28 hours of training in problem-solving and improvement techniques.

When Xerox first began its search for implementing TQM, executives paid to hear all the quality gurus and spoke with other corporations using TQM. What they heard and what Xerox learned from its experience is that each organization has to create its own strategy and develop a plan with employees so that it fits the company culture.

**Xerox came up with four core principles for its corporation.** Customer satisfaction stands alone and ranks first in importance. The other three are equal in importance to each other: achieving projected return on assets, increasing market share and maintaining a dedicated workforce.

**Xerox identified these core values.**

- Achieve success through customer satisfaction.
- Deliver quality and excellence in all things.
- Maintain a premium return on assets.
- Acquire the technology to develop marketplace leadership.
- Develop employees to their fullest potential.
- Act as a responsible corporate citizen.

**Xerox also has six enablers to produce quality.**

- Behavioral change for senior management
- Transition teams
- Training
- Modification of the reward and recognition system
- New communication patterns and norms
- Tools and processes

**Xerox used these tools in developing its "Leadership Through Quality" Program.**

- Communication and problem-solving training
- Benchmarking
- Calculating the cost of nonconformance
- Measurements of quality (specific products and processes)
- Management by fact (data collection and analysis)
- Mapping each process to create a "seamless" organization, where things don't fall through the cracks

**Former Xerox CEO David Kearns** was active throughout the process and assumed the leadership role with both integrity and pizazz. He made quality improvement and customer satisfaction the job of every employee. Today, salaried and hourly employees are expected to solve problems and improve product quality and customer service.

**Xerox sends out monthly surveys to 55,000 Xerox equipment owners.** From the responses Xerox learns what owners need and want and what they will pay to get the conveniences and features that mean the most to them. Xerox then uses the information to plan and develop delivery of what customers want.

**Team Xerox has more than 7,000 teams worldwide and says more than 75 percent of its workforce is active on one or more teams.** Xerox credits teams with saving $116 million by tightening production cycles, reducing scrap and devising standards and measures to improve processes.

**Xerox lists the following as direct results of its quality program:**

- 78-percent decrease in defects per 100 machines
- 20-percent decrease in service response time
- 40-percent decrease in rework
- Reductions in labor and overhead material
- Improved quality products and customer loyalty

The company's 1993 goals include a 50-percent reduction in unit manufacturing cost and a fourfold improvement in reliability.

**Xerox did extensive benchmarking on 240 key areas of product, service and business performance. The resulting standards came from world leaders in each category, regardless of industry.**

**Xerox's advice to those who implement TQM:**

- TQM is a top-down process with senior management a driving force.
- The organization will have to "mature" into TQM.
- There will be a change in the company's culture.
- TQM requires discipline and patience.
- TQM is not for the superstar leader who will not let go of control or the limelight.
- In TQM, everybody shines because they have to!

**When asked if a single division could implement TQM without the company already being involved from the top down, Xerox had these thoughts. It may be possible if the division:**

- is fairly self-contained and not interdependent with other divisions and
- has been authorized to act fairly autonomously from its corporate office and has the resources to achieve its goals.

However, the division focus will eventually compete with the short-term profit focus of the corporation unless the whole organization becomes aligned around quality.

## FEDERAL EXPRESS CORPORATION
## MEMPHIS, TN
### 1990 Baldridge Winner

**Federal Express has been aggressive since the beginning.** Fed Ex went with TQM because it wanted to maintain and expand market share. Founder and CEO Fred Smith launched the air-express industry in 1973. Within 10 years, Fed Ex was a $1 billion company. In 1990, it achieved $7 billion in revenues.

**CEO Fred Smith gave TQM full rein and drove the process.** He was visible and vital throughout and gave everyone room to participate. He outlined the guiding principles: people, service, profit, management by fact and analysis, continuous improvement and use of the Deming Cycle and philosophy.

**Training took on a special role at Fed Ex.** The company has a worldwide system for gaining input from teams throughout its network concerning how people are managed and what training people need most.  Morale is also checked. One of Fed Ex's recent report cards earned them a 91-percent "I'm proud to be a Fed Ex employee" rating. Fed Ex has a recognition program for both individuals and teams.

**Fed Ex says one of the most telling sources for relating how well it is doing is the Service Quality Indicator (SQI).** SQI is a 12-component, weighted index describing how performance is viewed by the customer. Daily SQI reports are developed from worldwide input. Quality Action Teams (QATs) work on the data each day and utilize 30 databases to locate root causes of customer complaints. Cross-functional teams work in introducing new processes. Teams steward the 12 service indicators to maintain their quality-improvement focus.

**Fed Ex has 43 percent of the domestic market, while its nearest competitor has 26 percent.**

## IBM ROCHESTER
## ROCHESTER, MN
## INTERMEDIATE COMPUTER MANUFACTURING
**1990 Baldridge Winner**

A dramatic increase in global competition and a need for a culture change from a technology-driven process of delivering new products to a market-driven one prompted IBM's sharpened focus on TQM principles.

**Six criteria guide IBM's strategic quality initiatives:**

- improved product and service requirements
- enhanced product strategy
- six sigma defect elimination (approximately 3 per million)
- cycle time reductions
- improved education
- increased employee involvement and ownership

Each senior manager "owns" one of the six factors and assumes responsibility for plans, implementations and monitoring progress. Hundreds of worldwide teams are in place. Quality goals are included in five year plans and in annual operating plans. Targets are determined from benchmarking.

## QUALITY IMPROVEMENT PLANS

Each IBM quality-improvement plan has an owner who may be either a manager or non-manager. Objectives are established, roles and responsibilities are clarified, inputs are determined, and a measurement system is developed in advance of the project to capture data. Both customers and suppliers meet regularly in planning meetings.

For example, more than 4,500 worldwide customers and business partners (suppliers) participated in advisory councils that helped develop the AS/400 computer.

## GUIDING PRINCIPLES

- Customer focus
- Total quality
- Global information systems
- Advisory councils
- Trials of prototypes
- Forty data sources analyzed to guide improvements
- Customers, employees and business partners all participate in solving the problems and making a better product and service

## TRAINING AND EMPLOYEE DEVELOPMENT

- Five percent of payroll is spent on training.
- Communication skills and working in teams are the initial focus.
- An on-line management system helps employees plan their education and professional development.
- An annual employee-morale survey supplies IBM with worldwide input.
- A recognition system supports the TQM environment.

## IMPACT OF TQM

- Thirty-percent improvement in productivity (1986-1989)
- Sixty-percent trim in manufacturing cycle
- Fifty-percent decrease in time for new product development
- Threefold increase in product reliability
- Increase from three to 12 months for product warranty
- Investment of $30 million for processing information systems to focus on prevention instead of detection

## BENCHMARKING

- Benchmarking at IBM is done through a worldwide analysis of products and services to determine the "best in the breed" in all industries.

## IBM's GOAL IN 1993

IBM's goal in 1993 is a 100-fold improvement and six sigma defect level by 1994. (Six sigma equals approximately three defects per million.)

# 6

## OPTIONS FOR THE FUTURE

Organizations committed to improving their productivity and pursuing a Total Quality Improvement Strategy usually want to know where to start. People learn in different ways, but when different learning modes are combined, retention and application are higher. The more people and the more levels of management that get involved early in the TQM process, the greater the chance for success.

As a manager or supervisor, you can influence how things happen in your own department. The key concepts in developing people to work within TQM environments have been presented frequently in this handbook. They are:

- empowerment of employees
- self-management and individual responsibility
- high commitment

There is no replacement for directly communicating and mentoring these values with your subordinates and co-workers. The fairness and commitment to quality of your working environment that your employees help create is the best foundation to encourage them to produce their best work. No matter what stage of a quality process your company is in, your employees will respond to your committed direction with respect.

Listen to Juran and Deming on tape. Try to catch Phil Crosby in a lecture. Attend seminars and watch videos with your team. Get your own people involved in a basic awareness of how TQM can provide an arena for continuous improvement and better service to the customer — both those inside and outside the organization.

List your favorite companies with whom you may want to benchmark. Who else in your business is already doing some of these things? Create teams to benchmark with these target companies.

Read Mary Walton's book about *Deming Management at Work* (Putnam, 1990) that describes how six companies are living quality. Florida Power and Light, the only American company to win Japan's Deming Award, is presented in Walton's book. PBS, with funding from IBM, produced a wonderful series entitled, "Quality or Else," in 1991. Lloyd Dobyns and Clare Crawford-Mason, who developed the PBS program and wrote a book under the same title (Houghton Mifflin, 1991), have worked with Dr. Deming on the 20-volume Deming Video Library. It is particularly effective for people who want to listen firsthand to one of the movement's staunchest supporters.

There are logical ways to proceed when you have gained enough up-front input. Who within the company will be the dynamos for the change process? Where will the opposition come from? Who do you need to get behind this initiative? Who are your mentors and soul mates? You will need them. The TQM road is a long one, although worth every mile.

Examine a simple problem-solving model. This may be more difficult than you might guess. A needs assessment employing McKinsey's 7-S model may be a first step. In investigating for TQM readiness, information is collected from everyone, using surveys, individual and small-group interviews, work meetings and planning sessions.

A diagnosis is made after an informed understanding of the current status of the company, division or department is obtained. Findings are presented back to an organization with the help of TQM and HR consultants, and much discussion occurs. The top team and second-tier managers are interviewed very carefully to get a clear reading of individual experience.

Various approaches and interventions are discussed. Who needs coaching? What will the TQM steering committee be given to do? How do you calm the misgivings of certain individuals? What needs to be done first? (This question is repeated regularly by TQM companies, so get used to it. There is always a new effort in continuous improvement.)

Developing a plan for sustained commitment is critical to the success of TQM. The early stages provoke high anxiety among employees. People are trying to find out if TQM will be worth it. Leadership has to be very clear and very supportive.

A steering committee is formed. Usually, the senior core team is represented heavily, and others from the second and third management tiers are pulled in who have the interest and the ability to participate in shaping a change process. They receive an orientation in TQM and usually take a refresher course in problem-solving and how to work in teams.

The committee works on developing its plan for action, and an assessment is made of other training and resource needs that the group has. Usually, one process is selected as a pilot for improvement. People are picked to work within that process. Data-analysis needs are determined and tools are provided. The objectives and goals of the pilot are clarified, and the cross-functional process team begins to lay out its own plan and strategy.

The organization will learn from the pilot and the early experiences of the team as it begins to benchmark and set its sights on improvement. The organization will have to be prepared to invest a lot of time and money in training. TQM is intensive in its high participation of people. In order for people to do well and experience success, they will need the skills and tools to go through a change process in how they work together and in applying new technical methods.

Measurement systems are important to gauge the improvements that are made and to understand just how they occurred. Operational training, planning and ongoing development and linkages with all new process-improvement teams are pivotal in creating the collaborations necessary to make TQM work.

As the company experiences success with improvement teams, the energy and enthusiasm will build. More people will want to get involved. There will be a new air to breathe — an air called quality. Quality with a common purpose will extend to include suppliers as partners.

Policy changes and new incentives will be required. Employee- and customer-feedback surveys will provide impressions and give ideas back to the organization as it advances along the TQM model. What was once a big mystery will become the organization's norm. Quality and productivity go hand in hand. It's no secret that people like things to work.

# READINGS

## SOCIOECONOMIC, POLITICAL AND HISTORIC

Chancellor, John. **Peril and Promise: A Commentary on America.** New York: Harper & Row, 1990.

Chandler, Alfred D. **Scale and Scope.** Cambridge, MA: Harvard University Press, 1990.

Choate, Pat. **Agents of Influence: How Japan's Lobbyists in the United States Manipulate America's Political and Economic System.** New York: Knopf, 1990.

Dertouzos, Michael, Richard Lester, Robert Solow et al. **Made in America: Regaining the Productive Edge.** Cambridge, MA: MIT Press, 1989.

Diggins, John Patrick. **The Proud Decades: America in War and Peace, 1941-1960.** New York: Norton, 1988.

Grayson, C. Jackson, Jr. and Carla O'Dell. **American Business: A Two Minute Warning.** New York: The Free Press, 1988.

Halberstam, David. **The Reckoning.** New York: William Morrow, 1986.

Kennedy, Paul. **The Rise and Fall of the Great Powers: Economic Change and Military Conflict from 1500 to 2000.** New York: Random House, 1987.

Morita, Akio, Edwin M. Reingold and Mitsuko Shimomura. **Made in Japan: Akio Morita and Sony.** New York: Dutton, 1986.

Naisbitt, John and Patricia Aburdene. **Megatrends 2000: Ten New Directions for the 1990s.** New York: William Morrow and Company, Inc., 1990.

Ohmae, Kenichi. **The Borderless World:  Power and Strategy in the Interlinked Economy.** New York:  Harper Business, 1990.

Pirsig, Robert M. **Zen and the Art of Motorcycle Maintenance.** New York:  William Morrow, 1976.

Porter, Michael E. **The Competitive Advantage of Nations.** New York:  The Free Press, 1990.

Prestowitz, Clyde V., Jr. **Trading Places:  How We Allowed Japan to Take the Lead.** New York:  Basic Books, 1988.

"Who is Them?" **Harvard Business Review**, January-February 1990, pp. 53-64.

"Who is Us?" **Harvard Business Review**, March-April 1991, pp. 77-88.

Rowen, Hobart. "Japanese Market Strength Is Detroit's Own Fault." Raleigh, N.C., **News and Observer**, Apr. 29, 1991, p. 1A.

Scholosstein, Steven. **Trade War:  Greed, Power, and Industrial Policy on Opposite Sides of the Pacific.** New York:  Congdon & Weed, 1984.

van Wolferen, Karel. **The Enigma of Japanese Power.** New York: Knopf, 1989.

## QUALITY

Albrecht, Karl, Ron Zemke. **Service America:  Doing Business in the New Economy.** New York: Dow Jones-Irwin, 1985.

Arai, Joji. "Productivity Experience in Japan." **International Productivity Journal**, Spring 1990, pp. 59-65.

Barra, Ralph. **Putting Quality Circles to Work: A Practical Strategy for Boosting Productivity and Profits.** New York: McGraw-Hill, 1989.

Cole, Robert E. "Large-Scale Change and the Quality Revolution." **Large-Scale Organizational Change.** Mohrman, Mohrman, Ledford, Cummings, Lawler, and Associates. New York: Jossey-Ball, 1989.

"What Was Deming's Real Influence?" **Across the Board,** February 1987, pp. 49-51.

Crosby, Philip B. "Criticism and Support for the Baldridge Award." **Quality Progress,** May 1991, pp. 42-43.

**Quality Is Free: The Art of Making Quality Certain.** New York: McGraw-Hill, 1979.

Davidow, William H. and Bro Uttal. **Total Customer Service: The Ultimate Weapon: A Six-Point Plan for Giving Your Business the Competitive Edge in the 1990s.** New York: Harper & Row, 1989.

Deming, W. Edwards. **Out of the Crisis,** 2nd ed. Cambridge, Mass.: MIT Center for Advanced Engineering Study, 1986.

Dobyns, Lloyd. "Ed Deming Wants Big Changes, and He Wants Them Fast." **Smithsonian,** August 1990, pp. 74-83.

Feigenbaum, Armand V. "America on the Threshold of Quality." **Quality,** January 1990, pp. 16-18

**Total Quality Control.** (3rd ed.) McGraw-Hill: New York, 1983.

Gabor, Andrea. "The Front Lines of Quality." **U.S. News and World Report,** Nov. 28, 1989, pp. 56-57.

"The Leading Light of Quality." **U.S. News & World Report,** Nov. 28, 1988, pp. 53-56.

**The Man Who Discovered Quality.** New York: Times Books, 1990.

Garvin, David. A. "Quality on the Line." **Harvard Business Review,** September-October 1983, pp. 65-75.

Gill, Mark Stuart. "Stalking Six Sigma." **Business Month,** January 1991, pp. 64-68.

Gitlow, Howard S. and Shelly J. **The Deming Guide to Quality and Competitive Position.** Englewood Cliffs, NJ: Prentice-Hall, 1987.

Godfrey, A. Blanton. "The History and Evolution of Quality at AT&T." **AT&T Technical Journal**, March/April 1986, pp. 8-20.

Holusha, John. "The Baldridge Badge of Courage — and Quality." **New York Times**, Oct. 21, 1991, p. 12F.

Imai, Massaki. **Kaizen: The Key to Japan's Competitive Success.** New York: Random House, 1986.

Ishikawa, Kaoru. **What Is Total Quality Control?: The Japanese Way**, translated by David J. Lu. Englewood Cliffs, N. J.: Prentice-Hall, 1985.

Juran, J.M. **Juran on Leadership for Quality: An Executive Handbook.** New York: The Free Press, 1989.

**Juran on Planning for Quality.** New York: Free Press, 1987.

"A Tale of the Twentieth Century." **Juran Report**, Number 10, Autumn 1989, pp. 4-13.

Karabatsos, Nancy. "Absolutely, Positively Quality." **Manager's Pak** (American Society for Quality Control), July 1990.

Kilian, Cecelia S. **The World of W. Edwards Deming.** Washington, D.C.: CeePress Books, 1988.

Kogure, Masao. "The Origin of Quality Control in Japan: The birth of TQC." **Societas Qualitas** 4 (3), July/August 1990, JUSE. Translated from "Total Quality Control," 41(7), July 1990, JUSE, pp. 58-65.

Lippert, John. "Cadillac Sets Sights on Quality Reputation." Raleigh, N.C., **News and Observer**, Nov. 29, 1990, p. D1.

Malcolm Baldridge National Quality Award application guidelines, available from National Institute of Standards and Technology, (301) 975-2036.

Morse, Wayne J., Harold P. Roth and Kay M. Poston. **Measuring, Planning, and Controlling Quality Costs.** Montvale, N.J.: National Association of Accountants, 1987.

Oberle, Joseph. "Quality Gurus: The Men and Their Message." **Training**, January 1990, pp. 47-52.

Pascale, Richard T. and Anthony G. Athos. **The Art of Japanese Management: Applications for American Executives.** New York: Simon & Schuster, 1981.

Pirsig, Robert M. **Zen and the Art of Motorcycle Maintenance.** New York: William Morrow, 1976.

Rifkin, Glenn. "Pursuing Zero Defects Under the Six Sigma Banner." **New York Times**, Jan. 13, 1991, p. F9.

Sanger, David E. "U.S. Suppliers Get a Toyota Lecture." **New York Times**, Nov. 1, 1990, p. C1.

Scherkenback, William W. **The Deming Route to Quality and Productivity;  Road Maps and Roadblocks.** Washington, D.C.: CeePress Books, 1986.

Sensenbrenner, Joseph. "Quality Comes to City Hall." **Harvard Business Review**, March-April 1991, pp.4-10.

Shiba, Shoji. "Quality Knows No Bounds." **Look Japan**, May 1989, pp. 30-31.

"Managers of Quality." **Look Japan**, April 1989, pp.30-31.

Taguchi, Genichi, and Don Clausing. "Robust Quality." **Harvard Business Review**, January-February 1990, pp. 65-75.

Walton, Mary. **Deming Management at Work.** New York: Putnam Books, 1989.

Wiggenhorn, William. "Motorola U:  When Training Becomes an Education." **Harvard Business Review**, July-August 1990, pp. 71-83.

Wood, Robert Chapman. "The Prophets of Quality." **Quality Review**, Winter 1988, pp. 18-25.

Zemke, Ron and Dick Schaaf. **The Service Edge:  101 Companies That Profit From Customer Care.** New York: New American Library,  1989.

## LEADERSHIP

Bennis, Warren and Burt Nanus. **Leaders:  The Strategies for Taking Charge.** New York: Harper & Row, 1985.

Bolt, James F. **Executive Development: A Strategy for Corporate Competitiveness.** New York: Harper & Row, 1989.

Callahan, Madelyn R. "Preparing the New Global Manager." **Training and Development Journal,** March 1989, pp. 29-32.

Covey, Stephen R. **Principle-Centered Leadership.** New York: Summit, 1991.

**The Seven Habits of Highly Effective People.** New York: Fireside, 1989.

Mills, D. Quinn. **The IBM Lesson: The Profitable Art of Full Employment.** New York: Random House, 1988.

Naisbitt, John and Patricia Aburdene. **Megatrends 2000.** New York: William Morrow and Company, Inc., 1990.

Raymond, H. Alan. **Management in the Third Wave.** Glenview, Ill.: Scott Foresman and Company, 1986.

Rhinesmith, Stephen H., John N. Williamson, David M. Ehlen and Denise S. Maxwill. "Developing Leaders for the Global Enterprise." **Training and Development Journal,** April 1989, pp. 26-34.

Schonberger, Richard J. **Building a Chain of Customers: Linking Business Functions to Create the World Class Company.** New York: The Free Press, 1990.

## CONTINUOUS IMPROVEMENT PRINCIPLES

Camp, Robert. **Benchmarking: The Search for Industry Best Practices That Lead to Superior Performance.** Milwaukee, WI: ASQC Quality Press, 1989.

Ciampa, Dan. **Manufacturing's New Mandate: The Tools for Leadership.** New York: Wiley, 1988.

Hall, Robert W. **Zero Inventories.** Homewood, IL: Dow Jones-Irwin. 1983.

**Attaining Manufacturing Excellence: Just-In-Time Manufacturing, Total Quality, Total People Involvement.** Homewood, IL: Don Jones-Irwin. 1986.

Hayes, Robert H., Steven C. Clark and Kim Clark. **Dynamic Manufacturing: Creating the Learning Organization.** New York: Free Press, 1988.

McNair, Carol J., William Mosconi, and Thomas F. Norris. **Beyond the Bottom Line: Measuring World Class Performance.** Homewood, IL: Dow Jones-Irwin. 1989.

Owen, Mal. **SPC and Continuous Improvement.** London: IFS Publications, 1989.

Schonberger, Richard. **Japanese Manufacturing Techniques: Nine Hidden Lessons in Simplicity.** New York: Free Press, 1982.

Vaill, Peter B. **Managing As a Performing Art.** San Francisco: Jossey Bass, 1989.

## MANAGEMENT

Associated Press. "Productivity of U.S. Workers Declines 0.8 Percent in 1990." Raleigh, N.C., **News and Observer**, Mar. 7, 1991, p. 10c.

Avishai, Bernard, and William Taylor. "Customers Drive a Technology-Driven Company: An Interview with George Fisher." **Harvard Business Review**, November-December 1989, pp. 107-14.

Burrough, Bryan and John Helyar. **Barbarians at the Gate: The Fall of RJR Nabisco.** New York: Harper and Row, 1990.

Buzzell, Robert D. and Bradley T. Gale. **The PIMS Principles: Linking Strategy to Performance.** New York: Free Press, 1987.

Byrne, John A., and William C. Symonds. "The Best Bosses Avoid the Pitfalls of Power." **Business Week**, April 1, 1991, p. 59.

Carnevale, Anthony Patrick. "Train America's Workforce." **American Society for Training and Development**, 1990.

Ford, Henry. **Today and Tomorrow** (originally published in 1926), Reprint edition published by Productivity Press, Cambridge, MA, 1988.

"How Companies Handle Layoffs." **Fortune**, April 8, 1991, p. 39.

Lawler, Edward E. **High-Involvement Management**. San Francisco, CA: Jossey-Bass, 1986.

Mintzberg, Henry. **Mintzberg on Management: Inside our Strange World of Organizations.** New York: The Free Press, 1989.

Naisbitt, John and Patricia Aburdene. **Re-Inventing the Corporation.** New York: Warner Books, 1985.

Peters, Thomas J. **Thriving on Chaos.** New York: A. Knopf, 1988.

**In Search of Excellence.** New York: Harper & Row, 1982.

**A Passion for Excellence: The Leadership Difference.** New York: Random House, 1985.

Schein, Edgar. **Organizational Culture and Leadership.** San Franscisco, CA: Jossey Bass Inc., 1985.

Scholtes, Peter R. **The Team Handbook: How to Use Teams to Improve Quality.** Madison, WI: Joiner Associates, Inc., 1988.

Srivastva, Suresh and Associates. **Executive Integrity:  The Search for High Human Values in Organizational Life.** San Francisco, CA: Jossey Bass, 1988.

Taylor, Alex. III. "Can Iacocca Fix Chrysler—Again?" **Fortune**, Apr. 1991, pp. 50-54.

# INDEX

American economic dominance, 15-17

Benchmarking, 76, 87

Crosby, Philip:
 four absolutes of quality management, 42-43
 fourteen points of quality, 43-45
 zero defect, 41

Cross-functional teams, 75, 76

Customer satisfaction and TQM, 9

Deming, W. Edwards:
 Deming cycle, 20
 Deming's obstacles, 33-35
 principles of total quality, 21, 26-31
 seven deadly diseases, 31-33

Employee participation and training and TQM, 9

Federal Express Corporation:
 role of TQM in, 84

Feigenbaum, Armand:
 six key points to quality improvement, 39-41

IBM Rochester:
 guiding principles, 86
 impact of TQM on, 86
 quality-improvement plans, 85
 six quality initiatives, 85
 training and employee development, 86

Ishikawa, Kaoru:
 quality control circles, 45-46
 role in business, 13

# INDEX (cont'd.)

Japan:
>	as economic superpower, 15-17
>	influence on TQM, 13-15
>	management systems, 14
>	TQM's influence on economic recovery, 15
>	view of quality, 16

Juran, Joseph:
>	Juran trilogy, 35
>	role in business, 20
>	ten steps to quality improvement, 37, 38
>	three points to total quality, 36

Knowledge:
>	components of, 22-24

Leadership:
>	as component of TQM, 73, 74

Malcolm Baldridge:
>	national quality award, 54
>	criteria for evaluation, 54, 55

Psychology, 23

Quality:
>	customer perception of, 10, 11

Shewhart/Deming Cycle, 24-26

Suggested readings, 93-102

Supplier-Customer relationships, 74, 75

Taguchi, Genichi:
>	loss function theory, 47-49

Team synergy/process improvements, 9

# INDEX (cont'd.)

Total quality management:
      benefits of, 2, 3, 8
      culture change as result of, 57, 58, 71, 72
      definition of, 2
      goal of, 1, 2
      how TQM companies work, 11, 12
      McKinsey 7-S model, 56-57
      origin of, 13-17
      readiness quiz, 58-69
      seven basic TQM tools, 50-52
      shifting paradigms as result of, 57, 58, 70-72
      TQM companies vs. traditional companies, 10, 11
      TQM management focus, 69
      TQM self-awareness checklist, 3-6

Win-win negotiating methods, 76-77

Xerox Corporation:
      core values, 81
      effect of TQM on, 81
      four core principles, 81
      "leadership through quality" program, 82
      six enablers to produce quality, 82

# OTHER DESKTOP HANDBOOKS

| | Qty. | Item # | Title | U.S. | Can. | Total |
|---|---|---|---|---|---|---|
| **LEADERSHIP** | | 410 | The Supervisor's Handbook, Revised and Expanded | $12.95 | $14.95 | |
| | | 458 | Positive Performance Management: *A Guide to Win-Win Reviews* | $12.95 | $14.95 | |
| | | 459 | Techniques of Successful Delegation | $12.95 | $14.95 | |
| | | 463 | Powerful Leadership Skills for Women | $12.95 | $14.95 | |
| | | 494 | Team-Building | $12.95 | $14.95 | |
| | | 495 | How to Manage Conflict | $12.95 | $14.95 | |
| | | 469 | Peak Performance | $12.95 | $14.95 | |
| | | 418 | Total Quality Management | $12.95 | $14.95 | |
| **COMMUNICATION** | | 413 | Dynamic Communication Skills for Women | $12.95 | $14.95 | |
| | | 414 | The Write Stuff: *A Style Manual for Effective Business Writing* | $12.95 | $14.95 | |
| | | 417 | Listen Up: *Hear What's Really Being Said* | $12.95 | $14.95 | |
| | | 442 | Assertiveness: *Get What You Want Without Being Pushy* | $12.95 | $14.95 | |
| | | 460 | Techniques to Improve Your Writing Skills | $12.95 | $14.95 | |
| | | 461 | Powerful Presentation Skills | $12.95 | $14.95 | |
| | | 482 | Techniques of Effective Telephone Communication | $12.95 | $14.95 | |
| | | 485 | Personal Negotiating Skills | $12.95 | $14.95 | |
| | | 488 | Customer Service: *The Key to Winning Lifetime Customers* | $12.95 | $14.95 | |
| | | 498 | How to Manage Your Boss | $12.95 | $14.95 | |
| **PRODUCTIVITY** | | 411 | Getting Things Done: *An Achiever's Guide to Time Management* | $12.95 | $14.95 | |
| | | 443 | A New Attitude | $12.95 | $14.95 | |
| | | 468 | Understanding the Bottom Line: *Finance for the Non-Financial Manager* | $12.95 | $14.95 | |
| | | 489 | Doing Business Over the Phone: *Telemarketing for the '90s* | $12.95 | $14.95 | |
| | | 496 | Motivation & Goal-Setting: *The Keys to Achieving Success* | $12.95 | $14.95 | |
| **LIFESTYLE** | | 415 | Balancing Career & Family: *Overcoming the Superwoman Syndrome* | $12.95 | $14.95 | |
| | | 416 | Real Men Don't Vacuum | $12.95 | $14.95 | |
| | | 464 | Self-Esteem: *The Power to Be Your Best* | $12.95 | $14.95 | |
| | | 484 | The Stress Management Handbook | $12.95 | $14.95 | |
| | | 486 | Parenting: *Ward & June Don't Live Here Anymore* | $12.95 | $14.95 | |
| | | 487 | How to Get the Job You Want | $12.95 | $14.95 | |

| **SALES TAX** All purchases subject to state and local sales tax. Questions? Call **1-800-258-7248**. | Subtotal | |
|---|---|---|
| | Sales Tax   (Add appropriate state and local tax) | |
| | Shipping & Handling ($1 one item, 50¢ each add.) | |
| | Total | |